Charles Robinson Bliss

Wakefield Congregational Church

A Commemorative Sketch

Charles Robinson Bliss

Wakefield Congregational Church
A Commemorative Sketch

ISBN/EAN: 9783337235932

Printed in Europe, USA, Canada, Australia, Japan

Cover: Foto ©Lupo / pixelio.de

More available books at **www.hansebooks.com**

A COMMEMORATIVE SKETCH.

1644—1877.

BY

REV. CHARLES R. BLISS,

Pastor of the Church.

—————

ἐ(hese are the Fathers.

WAKEFIELD:

W. H. TWOMBLY, PRINTER, WAKEFIELD'S BLOCK.

1877.

DEAR SIR:

At an informal meeting of the congregation, held on Thanksgiving Day, November 30th, 1876, immediately after the religious services in the Congregational Church, there was an earnest expression of desire that the sermon then just listened to, respecting the Old Pastors of the First Parish, as also a former historical discourse preached by you last June, might be preserved in printed form, for more general circulation and usefulness; and we were appointed a committee to carry such desire into effect, if we might with your favor and consent.

Pursuant to such commission and authority, and in accordance with our own sincere wishes, we respectfully solicit the use of your manuscripts of the historical discourses referred to, for publication, knowing them to be the fruit of much labor, thought and research—containing matter of great value and local interest—and believing this progressive generation may well pause a moment in its swift career, and gain new lessons in Courage, Faith and Duty, from the solemn Voices of the Past.

Trusting for your co-operation, and with feelings of high respect and warm personal regard, we are

Very Truly Yours,
LUCIUS BEEBE.
GEORGE R. MORRISON.
JOHN G. ABORN.
THOMAS WINSHIP.
GEORGE W. ABORN.
CHESTER W. EATON.

REV. CHARLES R. BLISS.

DEAR BRETHREN:

I have received your communication relative to the historical discourses lately preached in our Church, and sincerely thank you for the kind terms in which you have addressed me.

We honor ourselves in paying due respect to the memory and the work of the worthy men whose places we occupy; and, since the interest I have felt in reviewing the long and successful career of the Church is so generally shared, I cheerfully accede to your request.

Reciprocating your sentiments of regard, I am

Yours Truly,
CHARLES R. BLISS.

Messrs. LUCIUS BEEBE, GEORGE R. MORRISON, JOHN G. ABORN, THOMAS WINSHIP, GEORGE W. ABORN, CHESTER W. EATON.

INTRODUCTORY NOTE.

He who would understand the chief characteristics of the early life of New England, must study the history of her churches. The highest acts of men give to the world the best ground for an estimate concerning them: and the churches, absorbing as they did anxious thought, patient toil and unselfish endeavor, are mirrors in which we may see clearly reflected the characters of our fathers. Unhappily, they who make history do not always write it; and we therefore lack desirable facilities for tracing the church life of the Puritans. The records of the first church in Wakefield, though nearly continuous are not full, and are wholly silent upon various matters about which the church was with sister churches deeply interested. Yet they disclose a sufficient number of leading facts to give very clear impressions of the progress of the church, the character of the ministry, the questions which at various times agitated it, and the tone of belief and feeling by which it has been characterized.

This volume had its origin in the quickened historical spirit of the centennial year. A discourse upon the history of the church was prepared and preached, when it was found that the material at hand demanded another sermon. A Commemorative Gathering, to which the colonies of the church in adjoining towns, and the churches of this place, were invited to send representatives, was held, and speeches and letters

made the occasion memorable. It was, as previous corres-
pondence indicates, thought best to preserve what had been
rescued, and, as any change of form in the material prepared
would be attended with some sacrifice, the discourses, somewhat extended, are printed as they were preached. A brief
account of the gathering follows. Mindful of the pleasure
which the discovery of an exact picture of the church as it
was in 1676, or 1776, would have given us, we have attempted to give a picture of its condition in 1876 for the pleasure
of our successors, to whom we send herewith our cordial
salutations.

CONTENTS.

CONCERNING THE CHURCH.

JOHN 4, 38—Other men labored, and ye are entered into their labors.

This day is this scripture fulfilled in your ears. Look around you. Let your eye glance up and down these pleasant streets, upon these public buildings and private dwellings, and over these cultivated gardens and outlying farms; and then go back two hundred and thirty-two years, and look again about you. Rocks and tangled thickets fill the courses of these smoothly-gravelled highways. The public common with its graceful elms, the fields now leveled and fruitful, and the very sites of these comely houses, are wild with cedars and hemlocks; while marshes stretch hither and thither between these lakes, and the Indian and the wild beast dispute with each other the right to possess that which neither can hold. What a contrast is this! It is as wide as that between civilization and barbarism. Do we ask who were its authors? We are compelled to answer that we are not. Other men labored, and we have entered into their labors. What those labors were, in all their variety and difficulty and completeness, it were impossible to comprehend. Every generation performed its allotted share. The felling of the forests, and the organization and growth of the municipality, the school, and the church, proceeded simultaneously, and when one generation rested from its toil, its successor, with motives equally pure, and courage equally strong, stepped into its place.

Bearing in mind the variety of the labors of those first generations, you will not expect me to speak of all departments of their work. The accomplished historian of the town has produced an invaluable volume, in which municipal and social affairs are presented with great fidelity : but it did not fall within the scope of that work to trace the church life of your fathers. This, I propose, to some extent, to do. Should any one say that this is but the centennial year, and hardly justifies one in going back more than twice one hundred years, I reply—the value of the centennial year consists, chiefly, in the fact that it revives the historic spirit : and when one goes back as far as to the grand period of the Revolution, he can hardly fail to go back to the grander period signalized by the first consecration of this land to civil and religious freedom.

Not far from the year 1642, a small company of people, some of whom had just arrived from England, and others of whom had been a brief time in the country, left the shelter of friendly homes in Lynn, and planted themselves on this spot. Too few in number to form, at once, a church, they waited till the Autumn of 1644,* or that of 1645, when fresh accessions enabled them to fulfil their purpose. I will read to you from the ancient record, as traced by a hand that more than two hundred years ago "forgot its cunning," the names of those brethren :

Francis Smith.	Lieut. Marshall and his wife.
Mrs. Green.	Eliz. Wiley.
Will. Cowdrey and his wife.	Eliz. Hart.
John Pierson and his wife.	Lidia Lakin.
Bro. Dunton.	Eliza Hooper.
George Davis.	Zach. Fitch and his wife.
Thos. Kendall and his wife.	Will. Eaton and his wife.
Thos. Parker and his wife.	John Batchelder and his wife.
William Hooper.	Will. Martin.
Mary Swain.	Thos. Bancroft.
Joan Marshall.	Jonas Eaton and his wife.
Thos. Marshall.	Judith Pool.
Sister Martin.	Abigail Damon.
Thos. Hartshorn and his wife.	Lieut Smith and his wife.
Edward Taylor and his wife.	

* The exact date of the founding of the church is in doubt. In favor of placing it in the year 1641, there is authority as follows:—(a) Tradition in the church. Rev. Richard Brown, writing in 1720, mentions that year. The Bi-centennial celebration of the church was observed in 1841. (b) Johnson, the author of The Wonder Working Providence, published in

It would give us great satisfaction to know the precise spot where, with prayer and psalm and solemn covenant, they dedicated themselves to God and to each other. It was probably on the street now called Albion, not far from its eastern end. But to the genuine New Englander truth is more important than any dress it may wear, and covenants are more sacred than any places in which they may have been taken; and although we know not the precise spot where the founders of this church pledged themselves to each other and to Christ, we do possess the exact words in which they did so. Inasmuch as few of you have ever heard the articles which for more than a hundred years served this church as both creed and covenant, I will quote a portion of them :

"We give up ourselves to the Lord Jesus Christ, to be ruled and guided by him in the matter of his worship and in our whole conversation, acknowledging him not only our alone Saviour, but also our King to reign and rule over us, and our Prophet and Teacher, by his word and spirit. Forsaking all other teachers and doctrines which he has not commanded, we wholly disclaim our own righteousness in point of justification, and do cleave unto him for righteousness and life, grace and glory.

We do farther promise, by the help of Christ, to walk with our brethren and sisters of the congregation in the spirit of brotherly love, watching over them and caring for them, avoiding all jealousies, suspicions, backbitings, censurings, quarrelings, and secret risings of the heart against them, forgiving and forbearing, and yet seasonably admonishing and restoring them by a spirit of meekness, and set them in joint again that have been, through infirmity, overtaken in any fault among us.

We resolve, in the same strength, to approve ourselves in our partic-

1654, gives 1644 as the date. As he was an inhabitant of the neighboring town of Woburn, he would be likely to know the fact. (c) The early authorities of the Colony were opposed to the incorporation of a town till a church had been formed; and the town was certainly incorporated in 1644. In favor of 1645, the chief authority is Gov. Winthrop. He gives in his history Nov. 5, 1645, as the date. He is followed by Hubbard and Spofford. But he also gives the date of the incorporation of the town as 1645. Since the record of the General Court proves this to have been an error, it is fair to infer that he was equally astray respecting the date at which the church was gathered. From some source not easily ascertained, a mistake has been formerly made regarding the number of churches that were formed in the Colony before this one. Johnson, mentioned above, says that this was the twenty-fourth. The order was as follows:—Salem, Charlestown, Dorchester, Boston, Roxbury, Lynn, Watertown, Cambridge, Ipswich, Newbury, Cambridge 2d, Concord, Hingham, Dedham, Weymouth, Rowley, Hampton, Salisbury, Sudbury, Braintree, Gloucester, Dover, Woburn, Reading.

ular callings, shunning idleness, not slothful in business, knowing that idleness is the bane of any society. Neither will we deal hardly or oppressingly with any wherein we are the Lord's stewards: promising to the best of our abilities to teach our children the good knowledge of the Lord, that they also may learn to fear him and serve him with us, that it may go well with them and with us forever."

With such vows and promises, they might well anticipate what we behold in the fulfilment of the passage—"The wilderness and the solitary place shall be glad for them, and the desert shall rejoice and blossom as the rose." The fortunes of the infant church were, on the whole, prosperous. Its numbers increased, though its pastorate was, during the first eighteen years, twice interrupted by death. Though the early records are brief, they attest very plainly two facts. The discipline of the church was very careful: and its members were fully alive to questions in which all the churches of the colony were interested.

Every generation has its own peculiar and vexing difficulties with which to deal; and the first and second generations in the New England churches had their full share of them. The chief of these grew out of the unsettled mutual relations of civil to religious affairs. To explain this difficulty it is necessary to revert to a certain underlying idea which moved our fathers to come to these shores. Their ambition was to found a Christian state: and the best method of doing it awakened inquiries upon which the leading minds among them expended long and anxious thought. Their conclusions at length took shape in the principle which, in 1631, the General Court framed into a law that—*the right of voting should be confined to members of churches.* Mistaken as we now see the conclusion to have been, we have no right to impeach the motives of those who reached and adopted it. In the nature of the case, however, it could not stand. The requirements for entering the churches were rigid. There were worthy and conscientious people who could not enter them, and, what was still more portentous in the fears of the first members, many of their own children did not incline to enter them. Deep solicitude was at length awakened, not only in Massachusetts, but also in Connecticut; and a synod was convened in Boston in 1657, to examine the whole subject, and advise the churches upon it. The conclusions of that synod were unfortunate. Not seeing the wisdom of wholly separating church and state, they attempted to meet the difficulty by devising a modified kind of church membership— one to which Scripture gave no sanction, and one the working of which proved most disastrous. They decided that the baptized children of church members might, by a simple declaration of their belief in the Bible and the religion of Christ, without any experimental knowledge of religion, be accounted members of the church in so far as to entitle them to have their children baptized, which would also invest them with the right to act in public affairs.

This decision, involving as it did a wide departure from grounds previously occupied, encountered powerful opposition from the churches, and especially from the laity. Another synod was called five years later, embracing among its members the pastor of this church—Rev. Samuel Haugh— and the decision was re-affirmed. Soon, as we learn from our records, it was brought before this church for their judgment—for it was never the custom of the churches to accept any decrees of synods or councils till they had themselves examined them.

The propositions and the result of the action of this church are recorded as follows:

" The minds of the brethren being tried as to the practice of the children's duty to own the covenant in order to their children's baptism, themselves not in full communion—(1) It was propounded in a church meeting whether confederate visible believers in particular churches, and their infant seed whose next parents one or both are in covenant, are acknowledged according to Scripture to be the approved members of the visible church. (2) Whether the infant seed of the church, being members of the same church with their parents, are, when they are adult or grown up, personally under the watch, discipline and government of that church. (3) Whether such persons not admitted to full communion, being without such farther qualifications as the word of God requireth thereunto, yet nevertheless, they understanding the doctrines of faith, and publicly professing their assent thereunto, not scandalous in life, and solemnly owning the covenant before the church, wherein they give up themselves and their children to the Lord, and subject themselves to the government of Christ in the church,—their children are to be baptized. The propositions were voted and passed on the affirmative part. The brethren consented thereto by their silence, and afterwards by their usual sign, *nemine contradicente.*"

At first sight, the concluding portion of the third of these articles would seem to be sufficiently stringent to exclude all from the church, save such as professed conversion : but it was not so interpreted. The condition to full communion was a narrative of personal experience, describing the special reasons the candidate could present for believing himself a Christian. A formal act of owning the covenant, and acknowledging God, and submitting to the government of the church, was held to be consistent with the denial that one was an actual disciple of Christ, in the New Testament sense. Hence, a person could be a member of the church, while neither he nor others believed he was a Christian. In adopting this plan, those usually far-sighted men did not see that, in the process of time, many would be introduced into the churches who would have no sympathy with the doctrines preached : nor did they forecast the time, which actually came, when a wide-spread defection from the old standards would take place. Resorting to a human contrivance to strengthen the churches, they made them weak. With all they had learned, they did not yet understand that the fewer connections the gospel has with anything that appeals to the ambition or self-interest of men, the more vigorous will be its life, and the steadier will be its advance. But they were striking out a new path, and having the benefit neither of the experience nor the mistakes of others, their failure but shows that they were men.

Descend now one full century from that time. You reach the year 1765—ten years before the opening of the Revolution. Great changes have occurred. All the first settlers are gone, and the third generation fill their places. The forests have disappeared : comfortable dwellings have been erected ; and roads have been built. The first small meeting house has given place to one of more pretending aspect, standing a little to the north and west of this spot—a building already ancient and dilapidated, and destined in three years from that time to yield its place to the structure within whose well-kept frame we are to-day sitting. It is the 2nd day of September—a week day : but the church is open, and the saddled horses standing about the door indicate that some meeting is in progress. We enter, and find ourselves in a business meeting of the old church. The chairman is Dea. Benjamin Brown, senior, whose son, also a deacon, is destined ten years later to be a member of the first provincial Congress, a Colonel, and afterward a General in the army. The secretary is Dea. Brown Emerson—the grandfather of your old pastor, Rev. Reuben Emerson. There are Bancrofts and Temples and Nichollses present. We learn from their remarks that Parson Hobby had two months before departed this life, and that they had just observed a day of solemn fasting and prayer. They have now assembled to discuss a grave matter of church administration. From other sources we know that great uncertainty of religious opinions was prevailing. The seed planted one hundred years before was bringing forth its fruit. And this meeting was held to determine the proper answer to be given to two questions. One was—whether it would be safe for them to receive new members while without a pastor. And the other was — whether it would not be wise to guard the door of the church by a stringent doctrinal creed. I cannot repeat the speeches that were made upon that occasion, but I can state to you the result reached. As to the first point, they voted to receive members, but directed the Deacons to examine them and "receive satisfaction" from them : and decided that when such candidates were to be received, an ordained minister should be invited to administer to them the covenant. The second question they answered by voting that Ebenezer Nichols, Esq., Dea. Samuel Bancroft and Lieut. John Temple, should be a committee to confer with Rev. Peter Clark of Danvers, and Rev. Eliab Stone of No. Reading, and draw up, with their assistance, a Confession of Faith. Four weeks later that committee reported to the church ; and the creed then constructed and adopted is the creed of this church— unaltered save in two or three lines—now in use.* Whatever may be our general views about the usefulness of creeds, it cannot but heighten our impressions of the fidelity to their convictions of those men, that, without promptings from clerical sources, they attempted to stem the tide that was, as they thought, threatening the safety of their church. They took the responsibility that belonged to them ; and in the times of discussion, and rupture of old ties that not long after came to many churches, this was unmoved and immovable.

It may properly be admitted that the zeal for sound doctrines which at that time was becoming very strong in the hearts of many ministers as well as laymen, sometimes carried them to rather absurd lengths. An entry in the records, made two years before Mr. Hobby died, in his hand-writing, reads as follows—"Received letters missive from Marblehead, desiring assistance at the installation of Mr. Witherell, but being a stranger to the gentleman, his experiences and his principles, voted not to send." The next year this entry occurs—"Received letters missive from the 3rd church in Salem, desiring assistance in setting apart Mr. Huntington to the work of the ministry ; but, being unacquainted with the gentleman, his principles, morals and experience, voted not to send." Mr. Hobby was well known throughout the province as a disciple and defender of Whitefield, and hav-

* It has become so common among churches to recast their creeds, that it may seem strange that any church, professing to be abreast with the age, should content itself with a confession dating back 112 years. In reply it may be said—(1) The pastors and members of this church have never thought that their creed should be discarded, either because its language was becoming antiquated, or because some of its implications did not quite agree with modern theological notions. (2) The flavor of age about it pleases them. (3) The wise laymen under whose administration it was introduced were too wise to think that a technical creed ought ever to be used on the admission of members. For that purpose, they believed the covenant sufficient. The church has never pursued any other method. Each candidate receives a copy of the creed when he is examined, and, according to a standing rule, if he expresses no dissent before the time for his public reception, he is held to have given it his general endorsement. The church has never believed that an intellectual assent to dogmas should be mingled with a profession of allegiance to Christ. Hence, it has never felt itself forced, by the incongruities which others feel, to change its creed. Nor has it ever been admonished by the creeping in of heresies, that its method was unsafe.

ing suffered some persecution on that account, it was not
strange that he should be on his guard against endorsing un-
fit men as ministers; but lack of personal acquaintance with
them seems a poor reason why he should not sit upon councils called to judge of their qualifications. During the inter-
val between the pastorates of Mr. Hobby and Mr. Prentice,
the church, on one occasion, went so far in its solicitude as
to fail of its object. Having heard Rev. John Lathrop, they
liked him; but, fearing the leaven of heterodoxy, they passed the following vote—"That the church doth make choice
of Mr. John Lathrop, provided his principles of religion, and
methods of church government, agree with this church.
Voted—that the Deacons, with Col. Nichols and Mr. John
Temple and Mr. Nathaniel Emerson, be a committee to join
with Rev. Mr. Joseph Emerson of Malden, the Rev. Mr.
Robie of Lynn, and the Rev. Mr. Stone of No. Reading, to
examine Mr. John Lathrop." The result was favorable to
his orthodoxy, but not to their desires; for when, after
subjecting him to such an examination, they gave him a call,
he declined it. It is, however, far better that men should so
prize great privileges as to go too far in defending them,
than that they should lose them by prizing them too little.

It is quite impossible for Christians living in times like our
own, when denominational lines' have been drawn—after,
rather than before, theological battles—to appreciate the uneasiness of those living just before such division. Conscious
of increasing differences of opinion, and not knowing whither views thought to be errors, and yet vigorously defended
by good men, would lead,—such persons would naturally
become very wary, and at length grow so eager in the defence of important doctrines as to create, rather than heal,
divisions. After the death of Mr. Hobby, who seems to
have adhered to the position of Jonathan Edwards, that only
converted persons have a right to partake of the communion,
—a position then widely denied—a division arose in this
church, in consequence of which the celebration of the ordinance was for a time suspended. A brief record informs us
of the fact; but records are sometimes the more significant

for their brevity, and this is sufficiently so to justify me in quoting it.

At a meeting of the church, Sept. 1, 1768, Dea. Samuel Bancroft being Moderator, the church voted—"That, whereas we have for a considerable time past lived in neglect of the Lord's Supper, by means of some perplexing circumstances attending our affairs, we unitedly humble ourselves before God for our sinful neglect, and implore forgiveness through the blood of atonement, and grace for the future to honor Christ by a careful attendance on all his ordinances; and our purpose is, by the leave of Providence, to attend the holy supper with all convenient speed, hoping there to meet with Christ, and sit together as friends and brethren, forbearing one another and forgiving one another, as God for Christ's sake hath forgiven us." Fewer church difficulties would vex the hearts of men if such a spirit could be brought to bear upon them.

The position of this church during the early part of its history was one of greater relative importance than that which it has maintained since. Being the first church established within a circuit of several miles, it was the centre of more extended influences. The churches of Lynn on the east, Charlestown on the south, and Woburn on the west, were the nearest it: while there was none on the north. The people settling in that part of Charlestown now covered by the towns of Melrose and Stoneham, in that part of Lynn now called Lynnfield, and over all the tract embracing the towns of Reading, No. Reading and Wilmington, came here to worship. In none of these places, however, had the number of members increased sufficiently to justify the formation of other churches till the year 1720—seventy-six years after this church was formed. The membership of this had then reached 236—a larger number than it has ever attained since, till very recently. The year 1720 was signalized by the sending forth of two colonies—that of Lynnfield, and that of No. Reading. In 1729 the church in Stoneham was formed, and in 1733 that in Wilmington, chiefly from this church; while it was not till the year 1770, or 126 years after this church was formed, that the Old South in Reading was established. The formation of the church last named was a great grief to this. It took from it 88 members, among whom were many of the wisest and best of its number. It would now be thought very strange should any one suggest that the people of that town should come to this to attend church, for even some of our own school districts are thought quite too far away to permit their inhabitants to come hither to worship. But our fathers had different ideas. Physically, they required less nursing than we ; and perhaps their minds were less uneasy, their tempers less impatient, their faith more steady, and their principles better established. Certain it is, that exercise which was play to them is toil to us, and fatigue which they did not notice, becomes an attack of almost fatal disease to their children. They were, however, susceptible to the influences of inclement weather, for there is one entry in the record which informs us that, contrary to the pastor's wish, a church meeting was once held in his kitchen, because of the "sharpness of the present cold."

This church did not cease to enrich other churches when her own particular colonies had all been sent forth. It is among the arrangements of Divine Providence that some of the most influential things we do are those done contrary to our own wish. It was by no means a pleasant thing to the old church, but nevertheless it was a very useful thing, that the Baptist church in this town, three quarters of a century ago, took a portion of the strength and vitality of this body. The gospel as preached by the pastors of this church is in the very life blood of families which have furnished many of the most honored and influential members of that church. As a matter of church pride we should be glad if those families were still identified with us, but in a broader view it is no doubt better that they have been led to enter another portion of the common vineyard. There may have been, in former times, a rupture of old friendships, and a loss in some degree of christian charity and brotherly love, but, on the whole, the cause has gained. And if we can but preserve the unity of the Spirit in the bond of peace, the appropriate work of churches will be more thoroughly done, and the hopes of christians will receive a more ample fulfilment, from the divisions which a former generation witnessed. The Universalist church in like manner received much from this, though without its consent and against its protest ; yet for all the good which that church has accomplished this is quite as ready to thank God as though it were done by itself. Though there have been great changes in this church since its establishment, yet it is evident, from many facts, that the love of change, for its own sake, has never been one of its failings. Changes in it have been as gradual as those in the general habits of the people. Should you allow your imagination to carry you back one hundred and twenty-five years you would see in the pulpit a venerable predecessor of mine, Rev. Wm. Hobby, with powdered wig, and gown and bands. About him you would perceive an odor of sanctity and authority which the clergy of modern days find it quite impossible to obtain. The Deacons would be sitting near the pulpit in places of honor, and a flavor of sacredness, somewhat milder, but still very marked, would emanate from them. The congregation would be seated according to ideas of priority and seniority—the more grave and wealthy and revered occupying pews which the deference of the people had permitted them to cushion and ornament, while, in carefully estimated rank, the less rich and influential are assigned to seats corresponding to their degree.° Tithing men, ever ready to magnify their office, preserve decorum among the young people, and drive out the dogs. The scriptures have no place in the church, and are never read. One of the deacons reads the hymns line by line as they are sung. The sermon is from one to two hours long, and the prayers are but little shorter ; and when the service is over, the people retain their seats

---

° Under date of 1730, the parish passed the following: "Voted, That Real Estate and Age are the two first and chiefest rules to go by in seating the meeting house." Then they declared by vote that certain persons who had attempted to obtain eligible seats in contravention of that rule, were acting "disorderly," and ordered them to go back to their former pews. One of the men, not wishing to have such a stigma rest upon his reputation, brought the matter before the next parish meeting, and in consideration of the fact that he had years before expended money on the pew, the disgrace was by vote removed.

19

while the parson, with stately tread, walks down the aisle, recognizing by a formal bow the worth of some prominent parishioner, and impressing all but the irreverent with the solemnity of religion.

You need not be told that all this assumption of superiority and portioning out of dignity has passed away. But it faded out naturally. There was no foundation in political theories or prevalent ideas of human equality, for distinctions of this nature. Till the Revolution, there was a hope constantly asserting itself, and constantly proving itself futile, that some way would be devised to create an aristocracy in this land; and that pride which could find no other theatre went into the churches, and sought to create orders there. But the soil of this country never would produce certain kinds of fruit, and this was one of them. The levelling process began when the colonies were founded, and though many families with courtly ideas fought against it, the contest was useless. The Revolution was the culmination not alone of political theories, but of social as well. Powdered wigs were thrown aside. Formal distinctions that had lived with difficulty, died easily, and men, both in churches and out of them, came to the conclusion that the only thing that can elevate one above another is substantial worth.

But, though some things have changed in the administration of church affairs, others have not. You have already been reminded that the creed of the church is, almost word for word, the same that was adopted 112 years ago. There are other things that have had a still longer life. Upon the admission of members, as you know, we ask of them a written or oral public relation of their christian experience. This practice is unknown in many churches, and probably will be found in but few. Should you trace the history of it you would go back 197 years, and you would fall upon a curious record which states that some, having on account of some weakness complained that they could not make their "relations before many," the church was asked whether it would release them, but refused to do so. The liberal ideas of Mr. Prentice led, one hundred years later, to the suspen-

sion of the practice for a time, but the more conservative
views of Mr. Emerson, who followed him, procured its re-
instatement, and no one has interfered with it since. The
introduction of singing "by rule" savored so much of popery
in the estimation of some, that the pastor, Rev. Richard
Brown, ventured to favor it with great care. Under date of
1722 he describes with great particularity the steps he took.
The account will be found in the town history. Until one
hundred years ago the Bible, for a similar reason, was never
read in church; but the gift of a handsome folio copy by
Maj. Nathaniel Barber of Boston, led to the adoption of the
practice. Eighty-six years ago, the rule of inviting members of other churches present at a communion season to
participate in the service, was, by a formal vote, established.

For convenience in managing the government of Congregational churches, the practice has become universal of ap-
pointing yearly a Church Committee, charged with the duty
of attending to the spiritual interests of the body. This
innovation was made in this church in the year 1823. The
arguments for it seem to have been thoroughly canvassed,
and the Church voted unanimously to establish such a committee, defining at the same time somewhat minutely its duties.

Social customs always affect, more or less, ecclesiastical interests; and it cannot fail to surprise us, to know that when
Mr. Hobby was installed, the occasion demanded the pur-
chase of a full barrel of wine. It will surprise us less to
know that discipline for drunkenness, even when prominent
church members were the culprits, was not of rare occurrence. It was a long time before the churches understood,
if indeed they yet understand, that of all the foes of religion,
the use of intoxicating drinks is the worst.

This evil sometimes gave rise to nice questions of casuistry
in the church. In the year 1736 Brother Bryant accused
Brother Damon of slander in calling him a drunkard. A
church meeting was held. Bro. Damon persisted in charg-
ing Bro. Bryant with drunkenness. The record proceeds,
"Bro. Bryant, though he disowned the charge of habitual

drunkenness, yet seemed disposed to acknowledge that he had been overtaken with the sin of drunkenness, provided it might be thought an unchristian procedure in any to call him a drunkard upon such acknowledgment. Whereupon the church passed a vote that it would be looked upon as something unchristian and unjustifiable to call Bro. Bryant a drunkard upon his acknowledgment." He then acknowledged and was restored to "charity." The church assented to his proposal, that, if they would stigmatize it as unchristian to call him a thorough drunkard, he would confess that he had been a modified one. The church fulfilled its part of the contract; he fulfilled his: and the charge of slander was suffered to rest.

Some one has said that the best evidence of the faithfulness of a church is to be found in its records of charity. Judged by this rule, this church has been faithful. It remembered with generous contributions its poor members, its colonies, and other churches, even as remote as South Carolina. In recent times it has given liberally to missions, both home and foreign. During several successive years its charities have exceeded a thousand dollars yearly.

If christian patriotism be another sign of fidelity, the church has at various trying periods given it. A goodly number of its members are found upon the rolls of soldiers engaged in the French and Indian war, that of the Revolution, and that of the Rebellion. One of its prominent members—Col. Ebenezer Nichols—commanded a regiment in the French war, and another—Dea. Benjamin Brown—was a Colonel in the Revolutionary war, and afterward a Brigadier General. Several others attained the rank of Captain. The pastor of the church in 1775, Rev. Caleb Prentice, shouldered his musket, and, followed by many of his flock, participated in the Concord fight, while this meeting house served as a place of storage for a large amount of army supplies brought from Salem, and afterward removed to Watertown.

The church has enjoyed many revivals, one of the most memorable of which occurred in the year 1803. The parish had become divided in theological sentiments. Mr. Prentice, who died in February of that year, had preached the general system of religious belief that Dr. Channing afterwards elaborated. Though he was personally beloved by the entire community, some of the church did not accept his views, and withdrew to neighboring churches. He was, doubtless, sustained by the majority of his people. Before the year closed, and while a more decided advocate of liberal views was preaching as a candidate, the younger portion of the congregation were suddenly and mysteriously moved by deep religious feeling. The incumbent of the pulpit was not in sympathy with it, and sought to arrest it, whereupon, those who were awakened went from his meeting to one which a few people of the Baptist persuasion had just commenced. This movement alarmed the church; the candidate was relieved from duty; and a pastor was sought who should be acceptable to the new element. If it be asked, therefore, why a church that had for a full generation been educated by a pastor who was a Unitarian in theology, and was itself probably inclined to accept the same faith, became so strongly and vigorously orthodox, the only reply is, that man had very little to do with the matter. The Spirit of the Lord took it into his own keeping and decided it. Of later revivals, doubtless the most general and fruitful one was that in 1875, when sixty persons united with the church by profession.

The Church has been careful to define its position on various important questions. In 1832 the members voted unanimously to resolve themselves into a Sabbath Association based on the following article:—"Believing that all worldly business and travelling on the Christian Sabbath, except in cases of piety, necessity and mercy, and all worldly visiting and amusements on that day are contrary to the divine will, and injurious to the social, civil and religious interests of men, we agree that we will abstain from all such violations of the Sabbath and will endeavor to persuade our families and others to do the same."

In 1833 the church passed the following vote: "Believing that the common use of ardent spirit is inconsistent with the

christian character. Resolved that we will admit none into
our body but those who hold to total abstinence from it except as a medicine." As this position was taken in the early
days of the temperance reformation, it proves that the church
did not fear to be radical, if its conception of its duty compelled it to be so.

Congregational churches, though independent in one sense,
are not so in another; and this church has ever cultivated in-
timate relations with sister churches. The councils upon
which it has been called to sit have been multitudinous. It
has been summoned to churches far and near, to deliberate
on all sorts of ecclesiastical questions. The most prominent
of these councils was the famous one which dismissed Jonathan Edwards of Northampton, which will be noticed more
at length in the succeeding sermon. Rev. William Hobby, one
of the old pastors, was esteemed a wise man in his day, and
so onerous became the demand for his services that the
church voted on one occasion, that, as they had become so
deeply concerned in the difficulties of other churches, they
would not accept an invitation that had been sent them.
That there was weight in the voice of the church appears
from the following curious record made in the year 1748,
"The Second church in Ipswich being offended with the First,
and having, to no purpose, endeavored to compromise the
matter, then proceeded to administer letters of admonition,
which not answering the designed end, they proposed to send
letters to others, particularly to the 1st church in Reading,
(Wakefield,) desiring them to back or second the admonition.
Accordingly I laid the matter before the church, who, con-
sidering the importance of the case, desired that the matter
might be deferred till the next Lord's day; when, the consideration of the matter being resumed, not seeing sufficient
reasons to grant the prayer of the petition, they voted in the
negative." The church was ready, when asked by a church
to assist in settling its own difficulties, to do so; but when
asked to intermeddle in the affairs of another church, it understood Congregationalism quite too well to do it,—a decision resting on principles sound enough to justify them-

selves even at the present day. Under the pastorate of Mr.
Emerson the church was represented upon councils that in-
stalled Dr. Griffin over the Park Street church, and Dr.
Wisner over the Old South in Boston; and that ordained
the missionaries Hall, Thompson and Parker. Within a few
years it has been represented upon the council that installed
Dr. Rankin in Washington, D. C., and upon the Advisory
Council in Brooklyn, N. Y.

The method of conducting ordinations in early times was
different from that pursued now. The candidate preached
his own sermon. In the diary of Judge Sewall there is this
entry: "Attended the ordination of Rev. Richard Brown
at Reading. Mr. Brown preached well." At an earlier day
Mr. Pierpont doubtless preached his own sermon, since he
gives the name of Dr. Cotton Mather as giving the charge,
but says nothing about the preacher. At Mr. Hobby's ordination Dr. Appleton of Cambridge, a man of note in his day,
preached the sermon, and 37 years later he gave the charge
at Mr. Prentice's ordination. On that occasion the preacher
was Dr. Adams of Roxbury. At the close of the entries
giving the order of services when Mr. Hobby and Mr. Prentice were inducted into office, this sentence, in the hand
writing of each, occurs—"May he obtain mercy of the Lord
to be found faithful." Upon the council that settled Mr.
Reuben Emerson, Rev. Dr. Worcester of Salem, who probably preached the sermon, and Rev. Mr. Chickering of Woburn, father of our honored fellow-member, Rev. Dr. J. W.
Chickering, were called. At the ordination of Mr. Alfred
Emerson, Prof. Ralph Emerson of Andover Seminary
preached, and at that of Mr. Hull, Rev. Dr. A. L. Stone of
Boston preached. At the installation of Mr. Johnson, the
preacher was Prof. Austin Phelps of Andover, and at that of
the present pastor, Rev. Dr. E. N. Kirk preached, and Rev.
Dr. R. S. Storrs of Braintree made the installing prayer.

The time allotted to me is so far consumed that I must de-
fer to another occasion what I had intended to say about the
old ministers of the church. Reserving for that time brief
sketches of the first eight pastors, I will give the names of all

who have been settled here, with the years upon which they
began and ceased to act, adding notices of the later pastors :

				Began.	Ceased.
Rev. Henry Green,	-	-	-	1645	1648
Rev. Samuel Haugh,	-	-	-	1648	1662
Rev. John Brock,	-	-	-	1662	1688
Rev. Jonathan Pierpont,	-	-		1688	1709
Rev. Richard Brown,	-	-		1711	1732
Rev. William Hobby,	-	-		1733	1765
Rev. Caleb Prentice,	-	-		1769	1803
Rev. Reuben Emerson,	-	-		1804	1850
Rev. Alfred Emerson,	-	-		1845	1853
Rev. Joseph D. Hull,	-	-		1853	1856
Rev. Joseph B. Johnson,	-	-		1857	1860
Rev. Charles R. Bliss,	-	-		1862	

Rev. Alfred Emerson, after a prosperous ministry of seven
and a half years, found his health to be impaired, and resigned. Soon he was invited to become a Professor in West-
ern Reserve College ; and after remaining in that position a
few years, preferring the duties of a pastor, he resigned, and
settled in South Berwick, Me. Thence he was called to
Fitchburg in this State, where he was highly successful during a pastorate of twelve years. He now resides in Lancaster.

Rev. Joseph D. Hull did not remain long as pastor. Difficulties, arising from incongruities between that which was
old and that which was young, led him to resign at the end
of two and a half years. He became a teacher in Connecticut, and in New York City, where he still resides.

Rev. Joseph B. Johnson was a successful minister while
here. He, however, soon resigned and engaged in business.
Returning to the ministry again, he was settled in Uxbridge,
but soon entered into business a second time. The later
portion of his career has not fulfilled the promise of the
earlier.

During the administration of these later pastors, the usages and instrumentalities of the church have undergone

slight changes. The Sabbath School, established in 1818, fostered in its first stages by Mr. Emerson, became, under the superintendence of Dea. Aaron Bryant—extending over a period of thirty years—an institution of great value. All the succeeding pastors have given it warm sympathy, and depended much upon it. Prayer meetings have received great attention, and the causes of Temperance, Missions, and Charity under various forms, have absorbed much of their time, study and strength.

The church has adhered to the belief that Deacons should be permanent officers; and, among the forty members who have served in that capacity, a large majority have died in office. The number of members who have belonged to the church cannot be definitely ascertained, but it exceeds eighteen hundred. Of course I cannot speak of families that have from early times been identified with the church; of the Smiths and the Cowdreys, the Parkers and the Swains, the Harts and the Emersons, the Hartshornes and the Pools, the Wileys and the Eatons, the Damons, Batchelders and Goulds, and others equally honorable. We know less of them than we wish we knew, yet something regarding them remains. Their highest praise consists in the good work they left behind them. They found this spot a wilderness; they left it a fruitful field. They were a toiling, careful, frugal people, who prized possessions much, but character more; who loved independence, but gladly acknowledeged their dependence upon God; who had battles to fight, and in fighting grew strong. To suppose them destitute of failings would involve a grave error; but it would involve a graver one to suppose that they did not humbly lament their mistakes, and ask God to forgive them. They had their conflicts—civil and ecclesiastical—and, if they contended earnestly for the faith once delivered to the saints, it can hardly be denied that they sometimes contended for points in which the faith was not involved, and the temper of the saint was not illustrated. Yet their history and work prove that that which grew out of their sturdy English resolution; that which was personal and perhaps sometimes opinionated in them,—was, on the whole, subordinated to that which was christian and consecrated to the public good.

As we should expect, some descendants of those early families have become prominent in the world. We find in our list of Deacons three of the name of Bancroft—Thomas, Raham and Samuel; they were all lineal ancestors of Hon. George Bancroft, the leading American historian. Among our members is the honored name of John Boutwell; he was an ancestor of Hon. Geo. S. Boutwell, U. S. Senator from this State. Very early among our members occurs the name of Dix; Ralph Dix was probably an ancestor of Hon. John A. Dix, ex-Gov. of New York. One of our earliest Deacons was John Damon; he was an ancestor of Dr. S. C. Damon, now, and for many years, missionary at the Sandwich Islands. Thomas Parker was one of our early deacons; his Puritan orthodoxy did not, though his blood did, flow in the veins of Theodore Parker. Thomas Eaton was a prominent member of the church; he was an ancestor of Gen. Joseph H. Eaton of the U. S. Army. The lineage of several ministers of note may be traced into this church. Among them are Rev. Dr. Jacob Burnap of N. H., Rev. Dr. Aaron Bancroft of Worcester, Rev. Dr. Brown Emerson of Salem, Rev. Daniel Temple, missionary of the American Board, Rev. Alfred Emerson of Lancaster, and Rev. Frederick S. Wiley of N. Y.

The church has received at different times valuable tokens of regard from its own members. Legacies have been left it by Dea. Kendall Parker in 1755, by Thomas Burnap in 1773, and by Dea. Aaron Bryant in 1870. The aggregate amount of these gifts is now $1400, the interest of which is used for the relief of members of the church who need it, and for church expenses. Articles of silver plate have been given by Hon. Atherton Haugh, Lieut. John Pool, Dea. Nathaniel Stow, Peter Emerson, John Pratt, Thomas Pool, Kendall Goodwin, Dea. Jonathan Temple, Joseph Burnap, Jonathan Nicholls, Joseph Hopkins and Rev. Reuben Emerson. A few of the articles were, some years since, for reasons that were deemed sufficient, changed into other forms, but most remain as they were given, and all are in the church service.

The pleasure of going back over the records of a church whose history covers so many years is no common one. They reveal toil, suffering, joy, prayer, conflict and triumph. They admit us into many homes, reveal the secret of some disgrace, and explain why, while some families rose, others receded. They show how the prosperity of good men slowly increased, and how successive generations found growing strength in the same faith. As we read them, we trace in many channels the good results of the word of God. We see evidences of increasing charity, desire to do right, and care in balancing the scales of justice; and the conviction gains strength that a Christian Church, standing by itself, without aid from bishops or synods, is fully competent to settle difficulties, preserve harmony, keep the gospel pure, and commend religion to men. We gain, also, new impressions of the power for good which is lodged in the hands of a few christian people. By a wise direction of the affairs of a church, giving due honor to the institutions of religion, welcoming the faithful preaching of the gospel, setting before men an example of self-restraint, generosity, frugality, and Christian honor, they can do much to mould that public opinion out of which wise laws, virtuous habits, and sound principles spring. The worth of the gospel appears in a new light, and excites deeper feelings of confidence and gratitude.

From this rapid sketch of the history of this church we may well gain new lessons of fidelity to both God and man. While we do not worship our fathers, let us not forget them, nor leave incomplete the work they have committed to us. Their God is our God. Their work is our work; and may our record be as bright as theirs.

CONCERNING EIGHT PASTORS.

EPHESIANS 4, 11—*And he gave some, apostles; and some, prophets; and some, evangelists; and some, pastors and teachers.*

It was a mark of divine wisdom in Christ that he exalted that which was interior and spiritual, above that which was exterior and formal. Though he established a visible church, he yet so devised it that its strength should not lie in any carefully adjusted orders, or in any graded and balanced ecclesiastical authority, but rather in the truth of which it was to be the pillar and the ground. Nevertheless, he did not omit to provide instruments through whose agency that truth should be brought often and effectively to the minds of men. Apostles, prophets, evangelists, pastors and teachers, led by his spirit and commissioned by his providence, were sent forth as students of his will, expounders of his law, and preachers of the good tidings of his grace.

These terms, used by St. Paul, do not indicate definite and distinct ranks in an outward organism, but rather classes of teachers, often intermingling with each other, and to be employed as the circumstances of men, or the exigencies of the cause, might require their services. There are apostles now, if the word be used in its literal sense, to denote those sent forth as the Lord's messengers. There are prophets, if the word be used in one of its accredited meanings, to refer to those skilful to explain the truths of religion. And as for pastors and teachers, the church has never forgotten that if the gospel is to win the place it deserves in the faith and love of mankind, it must have a class of men set apart to declare it—men not specially inspired, nor consecrated by the laying

on of apostolic hands, nor dependent upon any alliance with
earthly power, but simply rendered capable by the devotion of time and energies, to expound the gospel, and justify
the ways of God to men.

The Puritans of New England adhered with great firmness
to this conviction. They esteemed the minister as, in some
respects, the most important personage among them, not because he assumed high prerogatives, nor because his office
awakened their awe, but because he was a more reliable interpreter than others, of the will of Him in obedience to
whom they had crossed the sea. The records of this church
afford sufficient evidence that its founders were abreast with
their brethren throughout the colony in their devotion to this
Puritanic and Christian idea; and its history, so far as light
is thrown upon it by the character of the ministry it has sustained, shows little departure from the ground taken two
hundred and thirty-two years ago.

Of this ministry I am now to speak. My plan will include
brief sketches of the lives of the first eight pastors, the last
of whom rested from his work at an advanced age, in 1860.

REV. HENRY GREEN.

This name stands first upon the list. The time and
place of Mr. Green's birth are unknown. On arriving
in the country he first went to Watertown. Being a young
man of scholarly habits, his services as a teacher were in
requisition. Coming to this place as early as the year 1645,
though not a minister, the church elected him to that office,
thereby asserting at the outset the anti-prelatical principle,
to maintain which they had left their native land. The proof
of this statement is found in Johnson's "Wonder Working
Providence." Sketching the origin of this church, he says—
"The people ordained *a minister from among themselves*—a
young man of good abilities and very humble behavior, by
the name of Green."* No account of his ordination exists.

---

* Cotton Mather, in his Magnalia, Vol. 1, Page 214, includes Mr. Green among those who

but probably, after the primitive method, the Deacons of the church laid their hands upon him, and solemnly set him apart to be their minister. The time of his service was short, for in three years he died. The place of his burial is doubtless near us, but the exact spot is not known.

REV. SAMUEL HAUGH.

Mr. Haugh was born in Boston, England, in 1620, and came to this country in 1634. His father, Hon. Atherton Haugh, was a man of some note, having been mayor of Boston, Eng., and came to our Boston as one of the Colonial Assistants. He accompanied his pastor, Rev. John Cotton; and though a pillar of the first church in Boston, he was a disciple of Anne Hutchinson. Tradition, however, does not say that the preaching of the son disseminated here the antinomian heresy. The son entered the first class in Harvard College, but did not graduate. With other boarders in the family of a Mr. Nathaniel Eaton, in Cambridge, he was subjected to severe discipline and short rations, and, having made complaint to the authorities, a suit, which was carried to the General Court and occasioned not a little disturbance, was the consequence; and one writer adduces this as the probable cause of his failure to take a degree. Be this as it may, the account of the affair which is given at length in a confession of Mrs. Eaton, which Winthrop details in his history, excites a good deal more sympathy for the boarder than for the host.

Mr. Haugh began his ministry here in 1648, but, in accordance with a practice then common and pursued long afterward, he was not ordained till two years later. The church then numbered about twenty members. and had just completed its first place of worship on Albion street. Mr. Haugh, who was a man of wealth, having property in Bos-

---

"exercised their ministry first in England," and brought the gospel to this country. As, however, he gives no facts about his having preached in England, and as he knew so little of him as to be ignorant of his first name, it is probable that his judgment was based rather on a surmise than a known fact.

ton, Cambridge, and Braintree, owned and occupied the ground on which the town hall and adjacent buildings now stand. The service of Mr. Haugh continued twelve years. Being in attendance upon the memorable synod which was held in Boston in 1662, he was seized with disease, and died in that city, at the age of forty-two.

We have from his pen nothing save his will, which is given at length in the town history, and a few pages in our church records. He was master of a very delicate style of penmanship, of which, however, if the reader would obtain the mastery, he must be very patient and somewhat inventive. Some of the entries made by him, while showing a zeal for church order and purity, might be thought to betray undue care for ministerial dignity. "High and ill language given to the Pastor," and suspicions that certain young men "laughed and jeered at the Minister," and an "offensive libel made and published by singing it," were, in his view, adequate reasons for resorting to discipline. His station in life, perhaps, made his ears too susceptible to possible slights. His style of expressing his thoughts was very accurate and pleasing, and the spirit by which he was actuated seems to have been a devoted one.

REV. JOHN BROCK.

The successor of Mr. Haugh was Rev. John Brock, who became possessed not of his pulpit alone. Upon an early page of the records we read this entry in his handwriting—"John Brock, called by the church to officiate among them after Mr. Haugh's decease at Boston, and dismissed to them from the Dedham church, was joined to them the Lord's day before ordination, and Nov. 13, 1662, he was ordained, and the day after, he was married to Mrs. Sarah Haugh, a widow indeed." Mr. Haugh had died less than six months before. We are not enlightened as to the reasons which led Mrs. Haugh to content herself with so short a widowhood, though we can easily see why she did not reject the advances of such a man as Mr. Brock. Alone of all the pastors of this church, he has arrived at the distinction of having his name quoted, and peculiarities described, in Cyclopædias and histories. Rev. Cotton Mather wrote a sketch of his life; and other writers, and especially the compilers of the Encyclopædia of Religious Knowledge, have made copious extracts from it. For the purpose of giving a glimpse of the writer of the sketch as well as the subject of it, I will quote some of its characteristic paragraphs: "Designing to write the lives of some learned men who have been the issue and the honor of Harvard College, let my reader be rather admonished than scandalized, if the first of these lives exhibit one whose goodness was above his learning, and whose chief learning was his goodness. If any one had asked Rev. John Brock what art he pursued, he might truly say—'My art is to be good.' He was a good grammarian chiefly in this—that he still spoke the truth from his heart. He was a good logician chiefly in this—that he presented himself unto God with a reasonable service. He was a good arithmetician chiefly in this—that he so numbered his days as to apply his heart unto wisdom. He was a good astronomer chiefly in this— that his conversation was in heaven. It was chiefly by being a good Christian that he was a good artist." "Good men," he continues, "that labor and abound in prayer to the great God, sometimes arrive at the assurance of a particular faith for the good success of their prayers. The wondrous meltings, the mighty wrestlings, the quiet waitings, the holy resolves, that are characteristic of a *particular faith*, are the works of the Holy Spirit. Eminent was Mr. Brock for this grace." He then gives several examples of direct, immediate, and special answers to Mr. Brock's prayers. Other men wrote of him in the same strain, declaring that he "lived as near God as any man on earth."

Several items in the records illustrate his earnest Christian spirit. He speaks as if with contempt of a certain difficulty between brethren, resulting in their "falling into a quarrelling passion over a few cocks of hay." He labors to raise the tone of piety, and enters heartily into the plans of the ministers to hold the churches up to the primitive standard. It was, however, in his pastorate, and by his counsel, that the mischievous half way covenant was introduced into this church. Yet it was then an untried measure, and one into which the churches felt themselves to be driven ; and they who see its disastrous results have no right to question either the integrity or the judgment of those who, having no light of experience to guide them, followed the best light they had.

Mr. Brock was born in Stradbrook, Eng. : graduated at Harvard ; preached at the Isles of Shoals : and came hither in 1662. He died in 1688, after a pastorate of twenty-six years, at the age of sixty-eight.

REV. JONATHAN PIERPONT.

The fourth pastor, was born in Roxbury, in 1665 ; graduated at Harvard in 1685 ; was for a while tutor there ; and was ordained here in 1689. Two years later, at the age of twenty-six, he married ; and it illustrates both the custom of the time, and his own filial spirit, to say that he did not take that important step till he had asked the consent of his parents.

The few records which Mr. Pierpont left of himself show that he was a man of clear mind, precise habits, and a deeply religious spirit. That he was a man of more than ordinary power in the pulpit, may fairly be inferred from the fact that he received at least five calls before accepting that from this church. A circumstance that had weight in finally leading him here, existed in the fact that, being present at the funeral of Mr. Brock, and seeing the deep affection of the people for him, he formed a high estimate of them. Mr. Pierpont worked effectively not alone as a preacher. Coming hither on the 28th of November, he appointed a fast for the 6th of December, another for February 27th, another for May 29th ; and on the 26th day of June, after a preparation of that sort, he was ordained as pastor. Like his predecessor, he was a believer in prayer, and made frequent appointments of prayer meetings with members of his own church and with neighboring ministers. It is a mistake to suppose that prayer meetings are only a modern practice in our churches. There were fewer stated ones formerly, yet, prayer meetings were common, at least in Mr. Pierpont's pastorate. Instances are given in the town history. Another is furnished me by the pastor of the church in Danvers, Mr. Rice, from the diary of one of his predecessors. Rev. Joseph Green writes, under date of July 2d, 1708, as follows: "I went with B. Putnam to Reading (Wakefield), to Dea. Fitches, to spend the day in prayer for him, he being almost blind, and old Mr. Weston quite blind, and other disconsolate and deaf. Mr. Pierpont began; I prayed; Dea. Fitch, Landlord Putnam and Dea. Bancroft then sung the 146th Psalm; and I concluded with a short prayer and a blessing." That the pastor of this church should secure the co-operation of a minister living eight miles away, and spend hours in prayer, to give religious help and comfort to a few old, deaf, blind and disconsolate people, is a fact that sheds a good deal of light upon the motives and character of the man. Yet this was not an isolated occurrence, but rather an illustration of a practice common with New England pastors of the period. Indeed, in a subsequent pastorate, fifty years later, there is an account in our records of the assembling of several ministers here, to pray with a man and his wife who had "fallen into an 'enthusiasticall' state of mind."

The death of Mr. Pierpont, in 1709, was regarded as a public calamity, and was mentioned in terms of great regret in the diaries of prominent men in Boston and elsewhere. He was but forty-four years old, and had been pastor twenty years.

REV. RICHARD BROWN.

Born in Newbury in 1675, and graduated at Harvard in 1697, Mr. Brown became an instructor in his native town in 1700, and continued in that calling eleven years, when he came to this place. He was ordained the next year, and discharged the duties of his office twenty years, dying in 1732, at the age of fifty-seven.

The most quaint and peculiar records in our church book are from his pen. His accounts of the establishment of a singing school, and of his anxiety to proceed in strict legal methods in church meetings, and of various matters of discipline, reveal him to us as a careful, perhaps whimsical, active and progressive man. His diary confirms this general impression, and leads us to infer that his feelings were devout and vigorous, though sometimes escaping the control of sound judgment. He had been here eight years when he copied the ancient covenant from records that are now incomplete; and the church solemnly renewed it. From the list of members then made, we learn that the church—which then covered the territory embraced in the towns of Melrose, Stoneham, Reading, North Reading, Wilmington and Lynnfield—numbered 236. Within twelve years from that time, however, three churches were formed chiefly from its membership—those of Lynnfield, North Reading and Stoneham—and the number remaining was 184. Mr. Brown, therefore, was pastor when the church reached its most extended influence, and sent out three of its five colonies.

The last entry in Mr. Brown's diary is characteristic of the man, and with it I will close my sketch of him. "Sept. 12, 1719. I am this day forty-four years old, and have received from God 44,000 mercies, for which I have made but poor returns. The Lord pardon, and make me thankful. I do humbly renew my love with God this day, and give myself to him—my whole self—and resolve that by his grace I will labor to live more closely with him."

Before proceeding to speak of the three succeeding pastors, a few remarks of a general nature may well be made. Each of the pastors of this church had his special rounds of duty to fulfil within the bounds of his own parish; but they were all in sympathetic connection with men outside their own field, and keenly alive to those general religious influences which, as every one knows, at times encouraged, and at other times almost convulsed, the churches of New England. It was, therefore, wholly natural that their position on certain questions, both of polity and theology, should be affected by external influences. Doubtless the first two pastors accepted the doctrines that none should be allowed to vote in public matters but church members, and none should be allowed to join the church save such as had been converted and baptized. But when numbers of moral and industrious men came to the colony, and, because not members of the church, could not vote, though paying as liberally as others toward the support of both civil and religious institutions; and when many children of church members were in like manner and for the same cause disfranchised, great changes of opinion upon the points in question took place. And the third pastor of this church, in obedience to the advice of the Synod of 1662, counselled an abandonment of the old ground, to such an extent as to affirm that a man of moral life might become a member of the church so far as to possess the right to have his children baptized—which would carry with it civil rights—by simply declaring his acceptance of the religion of the Bible, without believing himself, or being believed by others, to be a converted man. Rev. John Brock, when he thanked God that this church had unanimously approved that doctrine, was under the influence of external opinions, and acting in concert with the leading minds of the colony : and he did not foresee that the plan whose adoption seemed to call for gratitude would result in the admission of many to the church who could not give a heartfelt adhesion to Puritan doctrines, nor sympathize with the religious life that had been nourished under them. But laborious and earnest Christian men always do more good than harm, and, if in some respects they fail, God appoints to them successors, who, sustained by the good transmitted to them, are better able to withstand the evil. It was so in this church. If in the middle of the seventeenth century one pastor erred, in the middle of the eighteenth another was sent to rectify the error.

The sixth pastor, and in some respects the ablest man who has ever ministered here, was Rev. William Hobby. He was born in Boston in 1707; graduated at Harvard in 1725; settled here in 1733; and died after a ministry of thirty-two years, in 1765, at the age of fifty-eight.

Judged by his writings, he was a man of clear and vigorous understanding, extensive reading, strong purposes, and a devout spirit. Tradition says of him that he had a high opinion of ministerial dignity; was somewhat pompous; wore a big wig and large knee buckles; and was haughty and reserved. This may be true, but it should be considered in connection with well-known facts about New England society of that period. When royal governors occupied the executive chair in Boston, and His Majesty's officers disported themselves in the higher social circles of the province, and scions of nobility were possessing themselves of landed estates to found families, there was a strong tendency in all the towns to break up society into grades. The more wealthy and intelligent, with the minister, formed one grade; and, as there were no inherited privileges to assist them in preserving their superiority, they sought to keep the semblance of it by rules of etiquette, distinctive dress, and reserved manners. This was, therefore, rather the fault of society than of individuals. But if Mr. Hobby was reserved, his reserve was not assumed to conceal ignorance, or shield indolence. He was a thorough student, an apt and able writer, and an effective public speaker.

In the year 1741, Rev. George Whitefield, in his tour through the country, stopped in this town and preached on the common. Mr. Hobby heard him, and confessed that "he went to pick a hole in Whitefield's coat, but that the preacher picked one in his heart." He at once espoused the cause of Whitefield, and entered warmly into the controversy which followed the second visit to America of that famous man. The first visit had been welcomed by all classes; but the second was the signal for the outbreaking of an opposition as

violent as it was unaccountable. Whether, during the four
years elapsing between the first and the second, it had been
discovered that the doctrines preached by Whitefield were not
harmonious with those held by many of the ministers, or
from some other cause, it was evidently determined that his
path should be a rough one. Harvard College, though it had
before welcomed him, now entered the lists against him. Her
Faculty published their noted "Testimony," which was as remarkable for what it did not contain as for what it did. Its
writers had little to say in reproof of the low state of religion,
but much in condemnation of the preacher who sought to stir
up the churches. They asked for peace, but did not seem to
suspect that, through the half-way covenant, many might
have entered the churches, and some the ministry, who were
unconverted, and would naturally be excited on hearing their
religion called in question. They fell into the mistake of
condemning as a cause of divisions and heartburnings, what
was only an occasion of them; and, while Whitefield was
striking at the cause, they struck at him. Many ministers
joined them. Associations emulated them in publishing each
its "Testimony." Dr. Chauncey, pastor of the 1st church in
Boston, not only wrote, but travelled—visiting at least four
of the provinces, to counsel and warn the churches. Connecticut passed laws forbidding a minister, if uninvited, to
preach in the pulpit of another; and Dr. Finley, afterward
President of Princeton College, was actually carried out of
that jurisdiction as a vagrant, for breaking those laws.

But Whitefield was not without friends; and one of the
strongest and boldest of these was the pastor of this church.
He wrote a long, able and vigorous pamphlet in his defence.
He took up the salient points in the various attacks upon
him, and, in excellent temper, with some wit and great acute-
ness, turned them against his assailants. Many of his paragraphs are well worth transcribing; a few of them are as
follows:

"Does he not preach the same Faith, the same Lord, the
same Baptism? It is true, indeed, he is in labors more abundant, in zeal more flaming, and in success more remarkable.

And this it is which has made such an uproar, opened the
mouths of the profane, filled the secret hypocrite with indig-
nation and wrath, and, I fear, stirred up the corruptions of
many a good man. Such evils as these, as they ever were,
so I doubt not they ever will be, the close followers of enliv-
ened zeal and animated piety. . . . It is granted that
our Saviour came to set up a new religion, and that we are
Christians. But is the religion of Christ a new name, or a
new nature? If only a new name, I can hardly persuade
myself that the devil would have made such an opposition to
it. It would not greatly displease him to have Jewish men
and heathenish practices baptized by a christian name. If
the christian religion be a new nature, I humbly conceive
that it will stir up the resentment of hell at one time as well
as another."

Replying to the charge that Mr. Whitefield had said that
many ministers were, perhaps, unconverted men, he says :—
"I do not know of any tendency which such a reflection
ought to have in relation to ministers, unless to quicken our
watchfulness, excite us to self examination, and bring us to
resolve with the philosopher, who said—'I will so live that
none will believe my enemies.' As to any that have ques-
tioned the state of their ministers, merely on such expres-
sions of Mr. Whitefield, I never met the man. It is true, I
grant. when men have known their ministers load Mr. Whitefield with hard censures and severe invectives ; when they
have seen them bar their pulpits against him, which were
open to poor miserable creatures, while to them he appears
to preach the truth as it is in Jesus, and to be himself a kind
of living gospel—while this, I say, has been the case, many
have been brought to question the state of their ministers—
and I do not wonder at it. If Mr. Whitefield has insinuated
the idea that some ministers were unconverted, why need
they pave the way to the proof of it. He is not half so faulty
as some who, by their own virulence, have produced evidence for their own condemnation."

After admitting that most of the ministers were good men,
he says :—

"In a word, however honorably the clergy in general deserve to be spoken of, yet so many of them are of the contrary character that I think Mr. Whitefield excusable while he expresses his fears about an unconverted ministry ; and, while others are manifesting their angry resentments, I take this opportunity to express my gratitude to him for his concern about the ministers of Christ's kingdom, which I hope has been no dis-service to me."

He acknowledges that Mr. Whitefield has foibles, but asks :

"Shall I condemn a man because he is not perfect ? God honors him, notwithstanding his imperfections, and, therefore, so would I. In a word, I would do by him as God does by sinful men—damn the sin, but glorify the sinner."

Towards the close of his pamphlet he concedes the possession of proper motives to the men who had arraigned Whitefield, but adds—

"I hope they will pardon me if I express my fears that the measures they are taking to prevent schisms, disorders and separations, will be most likely to promote them. If I had aimed at the greatest confusion in my own church, I would have kept Mr. Whitefield at a distance ; but, as my pulpit has ever been, and shall ever be, open to him, we are, so far as I can learn, free from all danger of confusion."

Theological controversies often become more heated, and theological divisions become more marked, by causes that are not strictly theological. The so-called Unitarian controversy had for its source a radical diversity of theological opinion ; but he who studies it carefully, in its rise and history, will assign a place of no slight importance to the quarrel over Whitefield, as one of the agencies that, by embittering men against each other, and setting their supposed differences in a stronger light, paved the way for the disruption that followed. The fear expressed by Mr. Hobby was verified. The measures taken to prevent schisms, disorders and separations, promoted them.

The pamphlet from which I have quoted provoked heated replies, in contrast with which, it was a high-toned and manly paper. Its author wasted no time in controversy. His church, in common with many others, passed through a season of unprecedented religious awakening, which, doubtless, engrossed all his strength. When the fervor of that revival had passed away, and the charge continued to be repeated that the whole work was one of enthusiasm, he wrote, preached and published, a series of sermons designed to refute, indirectly, that charge. I will quote a few words from the preface to that book.

"Multitudes at present seem to think it religion enough to be no enthusiasts; and others seem to look upon it as an atonement for, if not a consecration of, the vilest profaneness, to level it against the enthusiast. In which task enthusiasm seems to be as little understood as it is admired; and, therefore, the soundest principles, the best regulated zeal, seriousness in conversation, and strictness of life, are branded with the name, and share deeply the fate of the rankest enthusiasm."

The volume itself is on the "Duty of Self Examination," and portions of it are every way worthy of re-publication.

During these eventful years of his ministry, Mr. Hobby obtained a reputation not only for soundness in doctrine, but for great prudence in practical matters, and was called to a very large number of Councils. The most noted of these were two which assembled at Northampton, in the years 1750 and 1751.

The name of Jonathan Edwards is honored wherever remarkable intellectual power and high personal worth are recognized. Though more than a hundred years have passed since his death, he stands without a peer among American theologians. But his evangelical convictions well matched his strength of intellect; and it was owing to his preaching and writings, more than to those of any other man, that the ancient life of the churches was re-enkindled. Nevertheless, the best intentions and the noblest service do not always save men from the hostility of others. Mr. Edwards preached that only regenerate persons should come to the communion. His people denied the truth of the position. He insisted; they became angry, and demanded that he should leave them.

He offered to submit the question to a council, on one condition. As the churches immediately about Northampton were thought to sympathize with his church against him, he asked that two churches from a distance might be summoned. To this condition his people at first demurred, but at length consented, and this church was one of the two chosen by him. The church accepted the invitation, and Mr. Hobby was accompanied by Dea. Samuel Bancroft as Delegate.* There was but one course for the Council to take. The feeling against Mr. Edwards was a tempest, and they could only advise him to retreat before it. Some of his friends published a protest against the result; which having been assailed, Mr. Hobby wrote and published a defence of it. A year passed away. The friends of Mr. Edwards in Northampton urged him to gather them into another church. He consented to leave the question to a council. This church was again summoned: and Mr. Hobby, with Dea. Bancroft and Dea. Brown as Delegates, again visited that town. The project did not seem to the council a wise one; and Mr. Edwards soon went upon his mission to the Stockbridge Indians, from which he was called to the presidency of Princeton College. Had Mr. Hobby possessed the privilege of choosing an earthly honor, he could scarcely have desired a higher one than that of being the trusted adviser and friend of Jonathan Edwards.

Mr. Hobby was a man of much native shrewdness; and many passages in his writings illustrate this quality. Among the incidents of him that tradition has handed down through a century and a quarter, is the following: He was the possessor of a fine orchard; and the boys, neither respecting his rights, nor awed by his dignity, appropriated the fruit. One Sabbath morning he surprised his people by delivering himself in this manner—"I am not going to have any more of my apples stolen; and, to prevent it, I hereby give full liber-

*See, in the part of this volume containing an account of the Commemorative Gathering, a letter from Hon. Geo. Bancroft, relating to Dea. Samuel Bancroft.
See also, for authority for statements regarding Mr. Hobby, and other statements made above, Tracts in Boston Athenæum, American Register, and Uhden on Congregationalism

ty to every person in the parish to take what he wants." It
is needless to say that the parson's apples found their way to
their rightful owner afterward.

That Mr. Hobby was a diligent observer of the tendencies
of theological speculation of his time, and feared the result,
is very evident. His refusal to sit upon councils, unless he
was personally acquainted with the candidates for ordination,
proves this. But there is other proof, in a curious document
which he wrote to his people, to be read by them after his
death. A voice from the grave, upon the qualities to be
sought in a new minister, he thought would have an empha-
sis quite too great to be disregarded. A few sentences from
that production are as follows—"Don't judge of a minister
as you do of a bell, by mere sound : watch narrowly his
preaching. Take heed what ye hear. Examine whether his
preaching be close, pungent and particular, or only large,
vague and general : whether by bringing in bad principles he
do not corrupt and endanger your souls, or whether he do
not cunningly conceal his principles for the present, that he
and his bad principles may creep in unawares together. Religion, I am confident, will be likely to live, as those doctrines which for distinction's sake are called Calvinistic, live,
or so die as they die. Guard against precipitancy. Take
time, and you will not only do it better, but do it sooner. I
solemnly charge you, as from eternity, that you do not lift
up your hands suddenly for any man."

I have said that Mr. Hobby was a man of vigorous mental
powers, and of much native shrewdness; he was also a man
of deep emotional nature. Some of the entries in the church
record prove this; but it is more fully shown in a published
sermon which he preached in his own church, before a regiment then about to march to Canada against the French.
The regiment was commanded by Col. Ebenezer Nichols—a
member of this church—and composed in part of the young
men of the congregation. He commenced his address to them
in these words—"My dear Brethren and beloved Children :"
—and then he pours out his heart in affectionate desires for
them.

The last years of Mr. Hobby's life were burdened with disease. He was laid aside from preaching, and suffered great pain. It was not strange that his people thought it desirable to settle a colleague with him; nor was it strange that, when he heard of it, he took it amiss, and expressed his feelings in a letter more emphatic than cautious. The letter, however, which is still extant, if sharp at the beginning, is kind at the close, and the records of the parish show entire friendship toward him. The following inscription may be read upon his tomb stone. "Learned, vigilant, faithful, he was a preacher of the word of God deservedly commended for his pure evangelical doctrine, replenished with erudition and piety, together with solid judgment and eloquence. Being at length worn out with studies, and with most acute pain of long continuance, and calmly resting on the will of his Almighty Friend, and earnestly pointing to his heavenly home, he breathed out his soul into the hands of his Saviour."

REV. CALEB PRENTICE.

Mr. Prentice, born in Cambridge in 1744, was the seventh pastor. Graduating at Harvard, he spent some time there as Librarian, and was installed here Oct. 25, 1769. He died Feb. 7, 1803, having been pastor here thirty-four years.

It seems to be according to a customary working of Providence, that leanings of opinion in one direction shall be followed and balanced by leanings of opinion in an opposite direction. It certainly cannot be said to violate the providence of God, that, in the town of Franklin, so long under the dominant influence of Dr. Emmons, who had the least possible sympathy with Universalism, one of the most flourishing schools of that denomination has sprung into life. The same idea received an illustration when, in the pastorate of this church. Mr. Hobby was followed by Mr. Prentice. Mr. Hobby had been brought into antagonism with the college from which he graduated;—Mr. Prentice was presumed to be in full sympathy with the college on the questions at issue.

Mr. Hobby adhered strenuously to the ancient doctrines of
the Puritans ;—Mr. Prentice accepted the modified doctrines
which have since developed into Unitarianism. Mr. Hobby
was a great advocate of revivals, and labored to promote
them ;—Mr. Prentice does not seem to have believed in
them, and trusted rather to the gradual effect of truth. In
short, they were upon opposite sides of the questions which
vexed the churches during well nigh a century. Yet, a careful study of their lives, so far as we possess the means to
prosecute such a study, will show them to have been equally
conscientious, laborious and faithful. If there was that in
the preaching of Mr. Prentice which, judged by orthodox
standards, would be likely in the course of years to make religion less vital and controlling, it was something that did not
seem to mar his personal piety, or make less urgent his desire
to commend religion to men. If we assume to say that he
had embraced, and was wont to preach, such views of truth
as tended to undermine certain essential doctrines, we must
also say that, judged by any standards which we have a right
to apply, he was a devoted Christian minister. There is
very slight evidence to be found in the church records, that
his views differed, in any respect, from those of his predecessor. The practice of requiring from each candidate for admission to the church, a relation of his experience, was suspended during his ministry, though the ground for the innovation is not stated. If it was upon the ground, insisted
upon by some, that it transcends the right of a church to examine the evidence for or against the fact of conversion in
any case, the change indicated an important divergence of
view from that of all his predecessors. That there may have
been other reasons is indicated by the fact that no other
change was introduced. The strong Calvinistic creed adopted a short time before his settlement, was left unmodified.
The Catechism was diligently taught, as few teach it now.
Sermons and lectures were carefully prepared, and vigorously
preached.

It was the fortune of Mr. Prentice to be pastor during
the Revolutionary war; and, having warmly espoused the

patriotic side, he marched in the ranks, musket in hand, to the battle of Concord.

Simultaneously with his entrance upon his ministry here, the Old South Church in Reading withdrew, taking eighty-eight members, among whom were some of the strongest pillars of the church, and leaving the new pastor to grapple with the discouragement of a great depletion, and the accompanying irritation and dissatisfaction. But the church recovered itself, and during his long pastorate enjoyed prosperity.

At the funeral of Mr. Prentice, a ministerial brother spoke of him as follows :—"He was meek and modest, unassuming in temper, and prudent in his inquiries after truth ; not credulous to embrace the first opinion that offered, nor unwilling to be convinced, on rational grounds. He was judicious in forming his religious sentiments. He embraced the Christian faith from conviction of its truth. From searching the scriptures, and from other sources of evidence, he was fully convinced of their divine authority, and that Jesus Christ is the Son of God, and the King of Israel. The gospel of Christ he received as the rule of faith, and the foundation of future hope."

Up to this period in the history of this church, all the older residents of the town have in it a common interest ; for, until the year following the death of Mr. Prentice, it was the only one in town. It had stood more than a century and a half; had gathered into its fold many members in successive generations; and furnished them the only church home they enjoyed. It was in the pastorate of the eighth and last minister, of whom I am now to speak, that the dividing lines of denominations began to appear.

REV. REUBEN EMERSON.

Mr. Emerson, the eighth pastor, was born in Ashby in 1771; graduated at Dartmouth college in 1798 ; was installed here in 1804; and died in 1860, at the advanced age of eighty-nine years, having been sole pastor forty-one years,

48

and associate pastor fifteen years longer—making fifty-six
years during which he sustained that relation. He was descended from Peter Emerson, one of the early settlers of the
town : and while preparing for college resided here. He had
the advantage, if it was such, of being known by the people
to whom he was called to minister. During the later months
of the year upon which the former pastor died, a revival of
wide extent and great power visited the place. The minister who had been employed to preach as a candidate for the
vacant pulpit, and whom many were ready to settle, lent no
sympathy to the revival, and even sought to change its
movement, if not to arrest it. His subsequent course con-
firmed the impression that he differed widely from those who
adhered to the old standards. Aside from the feeling produced by his attitude toward the religious interest prevalent
at that time ; a feeling of uneasiness on account of the doctrines preached, had long existed under the previous pastorate.
These facts, as I am informed by our venerable friend whose
head ninety winters have whitened, and whose memory goes
back to that time—Mr. B. B. Wiley—gave ascendancy to
the general sentiment which demanded in the next pastor a
vigorous type of Calvinism. There were other influences at
work. Opinions, both among ministers and laymen, had become sadly divided. The Unitarian controversy was rapidly
shaping itself to the separation that followed. The questions
between Baptists and Congregationalists were forcing themselves into prominence ; while other questions advocated by
Universalists were vigorously discussed. It was natural that
a church anchored as this had been upon the doctrines of the
Puritans, should seek a man whose opinions were of the Puritan stamp, and who had courage to declare them. Such a
man they found.

Mr. Emerson was a clear thinker and a strong reasoner :
and when he had taken a position he could not be moved
from it. He had a large acquaintance with the scriptures,
and could use them with great effectiveness. As is often
true of men of strong convictions, he did not fear controversy, though there is no proof that he went out of his way to

provoke it, or continued it longer than the vindication of
what he deemed the truth demanded. He employed much
of his time and energy in elucidating those doctrines which
pertain especially to the divine side of religious truth : and
wrote and published a volume for the instruction of his people. Several sermons of his were printed. Coming hither as he did when opinions were unsettled, and bitter
charges were scattered about by professed christians ; when
old land-marks were being removed, and new ones were taking their places,—it is not strange that a man of his mould
should sometimes have provoked the remark that he was
rigid and unyielding. But this firmness had its use. It not
only served to keep this church upon the old foundations,
but it brought out the characteristics of other churches in
bolder relief. If, as we shall all admit, God permits the rise
of different denominations in order to emphasize various
points of truth which no one denomination could sufficiently
emphasize, it is, in a broad view, well that the strong features
of each denomination should be made distinctly to appear.
Though controversy offends many, and strong characters provoke criticism, they are yet needful and useful.

The ministry of Mr. Emerson was a prosperous one. The
gospel was faithfully preached. The discipline of the church
was careful—extending with perhaps too close scrutiny to
mere opinions, but yet keeping the faith and lives of the
members pure. The pastor gave his warm support to the
temperance movement : but for another movement which
then attracted some attention, and is now attracting more,
he had less sympathy. It was, doubtless, by his suggestion,
that the church once voted that the sisters of the church have
the *right to listen* in church meetings.

Mr. Emerson was versatile in his talents. He was an excellent musician ; composed music, and sometimes ventured
into the region of poetry. Like his predecessor, he was
much interested in public affairs, and preached and published
sermons which breathe a thoroughly patriotic spirit.

From one of these, preached in 1839, I may quote the following : "Could my voice be heard from Louisiana to Maien,

and from the Atlantic to the Rocky Mountains, I would speak out with trumpet tongue, and declare as by prophecy, that subordination to civil laws in a free state can no easier be induced without the concurrent teaching of religion, science and morality, than the fundamental laws of God's empire can be annihilated."

Having become enfeebled by his long service, Mr. Emerson was, in 1845, provided with a colleague. The choice of the church and parish fell, with his hearty consent, upon Rev. Alfred Emerson, who was descended from the same Reading family with himself.

It is the testimony of the associate pastor that his personal relations with the senior pastor were of the pleasantest character. Perhaps the fact was owing to the spirit which prompted the following sentiments, which I find in the "charge" given by the elder to the younger, when the latter was ordained: "It is very possible that too much may be expected of us who are constituted co-workers in this vineyard of our common Lord. And who will not say—It is right that more should be expected than from one? I will tell you, brother, how we may clear ourselves in this matter. Employ all our talents at all times in the kingdom and patience of Jesus Christ, disenthralled from the world :— then, though Israel be not gathered, and we fall under the unsparing censure of misjudging men, yet, while these will find that a perverse tongue is a breach in the spirit, we shall find that a wholesome tongue is a tree of life ; our consciences will disabuse us, and we shall be glorious in the eyes of the Lord, and our God shall be our strength."

In the year 1850, the parish made an amicable arrangement with Mr. Emerson, whereby he was relieved of pastoral responsibility ; but with the express understanding that he should "continue to hold for life all the ministerial rights and privileges which he acquired by virtue of his settlement." After that time he rarely preached, though his influence was felt, and he bore the name and honor of the senior pastor till his death, ten years later.

Up to the close of Mr. Emerson's active service as the pastor of the church, in the year 1850, none of its ministers had ever been dismissed. Ten years later it could be said that the eight pastors, serving upon an average more than twenty-five years each, had all lived and died with their people. To the credit of the wisdom and forbearance of both pastors and the church, the record stands, that, for more than two hundred years, no difficulties demanding the services of a council for any purposes whatever, had ever been allowed to rise. Save for the purpose of inducting pastors into office, no council had ever been called. If dissatisfactions arose, they were suffered to subside, and the shepherds and their flocks went together down the hill-sides of life. The mortal remains of most, if not all, of those shepherds, repose near together upon a sunny knoll not far from the church, while on every side are the resting places of those whom it was their privilege to lead and to cheer.

In concluding these brief notices of the good men who have adorned the ministerial profession in this place, let me recall to your mind the thought with which the first of these sermons commenced. Other men labored, and we have entered into their labors. The outward blessings that we enjoy are not the result of brief and careless effort; neither are our social and religious institutions, our means of education, the truths we hold, and the sentiments we cherish. If with the Psalmist we can say—"The lines have fallen unto us in pleasant places, yea, we have a goodly heritage," the power to say it exists because men sustained and impelled by faith in God and love for Christ, have prepared our places for us. We are indebted to many men who have walked these streets, and established these homes—civilians of various ranks and of many virtues—but to none are our obligations greater than to the men whose careers I have briefly sketched.

Summoned to the ministry of Christ, it was their duty to guard the higher and more precious interests of men. They counselled the living, and buried the dead. They spoke in God's name on behalf of virtue, honor, intelligence and piety.

As the advocates of education, none labored more earnestly and wisely than they. As the friends of sobriety and order,

none wielded greater moral power than they. As the pro-
moters of right feeling and sound principles in society, the
influence of none surpassed theirs. Their honored position,
the truths which they declared, and the worth of their personal characters, made their continued labors a source of pos-
itive power in the defence of righteousness, and the promotion
of real prosperity. True to the spirit of their office, they
proclaimed Christ to men, and with his aid evoked in many
hearts high resolves, pure desires, and divine affections.
They made full proof of their ministry; and, though dead,
they yet speak to us, and commend anew the truth which
through two centuries has filled these homes with light.

It would have been unpatriotic to allow the centennial year
to pass without due recognition. The method of giving it
fit honor, though for a time in doubt, was satisfactorily settled. As the pastor who served the church in 1776, hastened
with not a few of his flock to the Concord battle ; and as the
present meeting-house—still comely, massive and sound in
all its timbers—is the very structure in which supplies for
the army of Washington were stored,—it was deemed quite
proper that the church should draw the plan of the observ-
ance. The only objection was that she was too old. This,
however, was over-ruled, on the ground that, though she
had been at work more than a century and a quarter before
the Revolution, and had never rested since, her spirit was as
young as ever. The plan which she ventured to suggest,
included two hundred and thirty-two years, rather than one
hundred, and was executed nearly in the following manner :

On the evening of Wednesday, June 21st, 1876, a large
company assembled at the church. Invited guests from other
towns and churches, and representatives of old families, were
present in goodly numbers. Many of the ladies and gentlemen wore antique costumes, and a great variety of relics
of past days and usages were displayed. After an hour
spent in social intercourse, the company was called to order
by E. W. Eaton, Esq., who introduced the president of the
occasion—S. K. Hamilton, Esq. After extending a cordial
welcome to the assembled guests, he invited them to repair
to the tastefully adorned vestries. Under the direction of
Mr. A. A. Currier, ample tables for four hundred guests had
been spread, and every seat was filled. The enthusiastic
singing of America, and a fervent prayer, opened the exer-

cises. The abundant repast having been finished, and the audience having listened to excellent singing, the President spoke as follows:

ADDRESS OF MR. HAMILTON.

I count it high honor to-night, to welcome this presence to its ancestral home; to welcome these representatives of those pious and sturdy men who planted this church in the wilderness, and defended it with their blood,—these representatives who have assembled on the old spot to revive the memories of the centuries gone by; to recount the more than heroic deeds of the fathers, and perchance to draw inspiration from their history. From whatever quarter you come, or however related to the old church or to the fathers, whether by lineal or lateral ties, or only by right of representation—I bid you a cordial welcome—*thrice* welcome.

This year the nation celebrates its hundredth birthday by an exposition, it is only trite to say, the like whereof the world has never seen. The whole country—from the farthest north to the Gulf, from the Atlantic slope to the Golden Gate—gives of its vast resources to the National Jubilation. The choicest products of her agriculture, her mechanics, her arts, her sciences and her literature, have been culled to show her progress, and establish her place. The old world—even the farthest East—has sent from her workshop its best handiwork; from her loom its finest fabric; and from her easel its most artistic touch, to grace the occasion—and even the sea has given of its glories to add splendor to the scene.

It is, too, a harvest year in rebellious incidents and revolutionary memories, when the nation and individuals are greedily garnering up whatever relates to national or individual history of "the times that tried men's souls."

It is well for this church, which had arrived at a patriarchal age when the nation was born, and which took an active part in the great struggle which gave it place among the nations, to gather up its traditions, bring forth its relics, and recite what it can of the local events which have transpired during the two hundred and thirty-two years which it has lived—and to keep fresh in our hearts the memories of those men who planted here the seeds of the civil and religious liberty which we now enjoy; who endured trial and danger, privation and suffering, that they and those who came after them might enjoy what the monarchs of the old world denied—a right to worship God according to the dictates of their own consciences.

We, of this day and generation, surrounded by all the blessings which their labor purchased, can have but faint conception of their cost. We cannot realize the deprivation and suffering incident to founding a colony and a nation in a land whose only inhabitants are wild beasts and wilder savages—whose every bush and rock is a lurking place for the foe. Nor can we realize the deep conviction or the patriotic devotion which could sustain a long and successful revolution for the sake of a principle—but we can recall the stirring events of those times, and revive the motives which prompted them; and we can detect the vital principles of both their civil and religious polity—love of God, liberty of conscience, just and equal laws made by all the people, for the general good—an enunciation of civil, political and religious doctrine second only to that written by the finger of God on tablets of stone. By assembling, and recalling their deeds and motives, we can the better enjoy those inestimable blessings which flow from their labors, and the better transmit them to those who come after us. In these times, when the nation, as well as individuals, lives upon the high pressure system, when progress is the only watchword, we are in danger of drifting away from our anchorage ground. In our great haste for wealth and place, we are in danger of losing sight of the great truths which lie at the basis of our success. We have seen it in business, and, alas, we have seen it in politics, where, next to his own family, a man ought to be pure; we have seen it in law, and I fear we may see it in religion, unless we take anew our bearings, and anchor our belief on the Puritan Rock.

I see here before me descendants of the oldest families, of the men who felled the first trees in the unbroken forest; who laid the corner stone of this church, and signed the first compact; descendants, also, of those God fearing men "who took their lives in their hands, and perilled their all in the sacred cause of freedom." On you I call to-night for the tradition of your families, for the legends which have descended from generation to generation, for whatever you may know of church or individual history. Tell it to us in speech or song, in prose or verse, as the heart may prompt.

I will now introduce to you a gentleman descended from one of our oldest families, who, to the antiquarian love that he inherits, adds the qualities of wisdom and wit; and who, as Toastmaster, will exercise his skill in calling forth the speeches which some of you are competent to deliver, and all of you are waiting to hear—

C. W. EATON, ESQ.

In the applause which followed the address, Mr. Eaton arose, and after a few words expressive of his pleasure in the occasion, proceeded in the discharge of his duty, to read

THE FIRST SENTIMENT:

The Church of the First Parish—Consecrated by Time, may it more rejoice in a consecration from on high. During the centuries it has stood a citadel for the right;—may it remain while time shall last, a tower strong in truth, and Heaven's beacon for the wandering and the lost. It has been divinely guided and instructed, through a succession of able and devoted Christian ministers, from Rev. Henry Green, in 1645, to Rev. Charles R. Bliss, in 1876.

THE RESPONSE OF MR. BLISS.

I shall beg your forbearance if I find it impossible to express what the occasion demands of me. Most cordially do I welcome you, and most heartily do I thank you for your presence. The honors of the evening belong not to the pastor, but to the church. One of the first institutions ever planted by civilized man on this spot, it has had a history of growth and usefulness which may well excite the deepest pleasure and the liveliest gratitude. For seventy-five years it was the only religious beacon from Charlestown to the Merrimac, and into many a settler's lowly cabin, and into many a weary heart, did it shed the light of faith and hope. Sending forth its colonies one by one, it upheld them, and wrought, through their hands, while it wielded a more concentrated influence in its own narrowed sphere.

Its first eight pastors, covering with their faithful service two full centuries, left a record of their work where time cannot efface it. Nourishing this church in its infancy, and guiding its energies in later years, they helped to make it an ally of good order, and a promoter of righteousness, whose influence this community feels in every nerve. The spirit of independence—shared by your fathers, as records prove, to the full measure of patriotic devotion—found in this church one source of its inspiration. The love of education—the just pride of our community —exists in its strength because this church and parish charged themselves with the duty of providing public instruction for the children. Respect for law—"the second nature of New Englanders," and as vigorous here as in any community beneath the sun—derives a portion of its vitality from the Calvinistic views of divine law which this pulpit proclaimed. A church, historic like this—having grown with the institutions around it, and uttered its voice on all important questions, and exerted the influence of its doctrines, principles and spirit, from age to age, through a thousand channels—wields, and must wield, a power not to be traced or measured by finite minds.

Let me congratulate you that so many churches exist where once this held up alone the banner of Christ. We rejoice in their number, strength and prosperity. Could the faithful men and women who planted in the wilderness the seed from which these erect and beautiful growths have

sprung, look upon them now, their astonishment would baffle the power
of expression. Like a bright vision of Hebrew prophecy would this
hour of festivity gleam on their sight. It is their honor, that the
work given them was thoroughly done; and well may we perpetuate
their memories. To this glad task let me again welcome you. We
greet with joy the daughters of this honored mother; the neighbors who
live on terms of unfeigned amity with her, and the numerous guests
before us, who manifest by their presence kind thoughts of her. May the
God of the Fathers protect the children, and may our work bear to our
successors the evidence of christian wisdom, zeal and fidelity.

The Banian tree, with its numerous trunks and perpetual life, is regarded
by the Hindoos as an emblem of Deity. An ancient christian church, vital with spiritual life, is often like that wide-spreading tree. Its extending branches falling to the ground, taking root and rising again as new
trunks, not only support the parent stock and increase its beauty, but cover wide spaces with the refreshing shade of religious truth. The earliest
branch of THIS Banian tree fell northward, touching the soil in 1713, and
sending its roots firmly down in 1720. We shall ask our brethren of
North Reading to tell us how large that trunk has become, and how se-
curely it stands; or, to express our feelings more accurately, we will ask
the eldest daughter to report her prosperity.

The Rev. J. W. Kingsbury, pastor at North Reading, responded:

Mr. CHAIRMAN: I am glad that the church I have the pleasure to
represent had so good a mother—so much, you know, depends on good
early training. I am glad, too, that when our church went away she departed not as the Prodigal Son, to waste her substance in riotous living
in a far country, but as a prudent and well-beloved elder daughter, with
the parental blessing resting upon her, went to her humble home in
what was then a part of the same town, there to imitate the virtues and
piety of the good mother.

With heartfelt gratitude the elder daughter recalls how, in all her history and in all her trials, this mother church has followed her with un-
ceasing interest and sympathy, and through one channel or another is
helping her to bear the burden and heat of the day; and at every family gathering, or festive occasion, has for her a welcome and a place.
By reference to what we may call the Family Record, I find that when
the elder daughter began life and housekeeping—for, strange as it may
seem, she began them together—our venerable mother was 75 years
old. I learn, too, that when a half century had passed, and consequent-
ly when our mother was much older than Abraham's wife, she was

blessed with another daughter. But this younger daughter must have grown old fast, or she would not have been called "*Old South.*" However, she was vigorous enough in her 80th year to give birth to a child named "Bethesda."

While the Family Record and the fact of grandmotherhood afford convincing proof of the venerable age of the mother church, yet her 232 years rest lightly upon her, and we joyfully perceive that her eye is not dim, nor her natural force abated.

We gladly yield to her the palm for experience and wisdom, for vigor and activity; and feel that it is no disparagement to any of her offspring, to apply to her Milton's description of Eve, and declare her the "fairest of her daughters." With these other daughters, in whose larger success the elder rejoices, we are glad here this evening to rise up and call our mother blessed. For her we invoke the blessing invoked upon Rebekah by her kindred—"Be thou the mother of thousands of millions, and let thy seed possess the gate of those which hate them." Good mother, long may you live, and long remain your present "Bliss."

The second branch of this Banian fell slightly toward the northeast, and also became fast as a new trunk in 1720. Our Lynnfield brethren are requested to report the girth and strength and beauty of it; or to inform us what fortunes the second daughter has met.

Rev. D. B. Scott, pastor of the church at Lynnfield, responded.

Mr. President, Ladies and Gentlemen: The church in Lynnfield has not forgotten her mother. It is said that the metropolitan question in Boston is, "How much do you *know*"—in New York, "How much *money* have you got"—in Philadelphia, "Who are your *ancestors.*" Like the Philadelphians, the church in Lynnfield talks about her ancestors. She has been in perils by false teachers; and been compelled to choose between submission to hands that would take the crown of divinity from the Redeemer's head, or go out. She remained true "to the faith once delivered to the saints," and the members "went out, not knowing whither they went." Now they have a house of worship, a membership of 75, and a zeal for God that is "according to knowledge."

The churches of Stoneham and Wilmington had been duly invited, and sentiments in their honor were offered; but being, perhaps, enlisted in other centennial projects, their representatives were not present.

Nothing is more comely than the relations existing between a mother of ripe age, courtly in manner and kindly in spirit, and a daughter grown to mature womanhood, also a mother, and equally imbued with generous feeling. Having long been companions, they are rather sisters than mother and daughter. Mutual affection and confidence remove every vestige of occasional disagreement, and they pursue the even tenor of their way loving and beloved. Such relations sometimes exist between churches. This church and the Old South Church in Reading, for more than one hundred years have walked together and leaned upon each other. If this church claims the honors of motherhood, it is but to emphasize the pride with which she points to her daughter.

The representatives of the Old South church, now without a pastor, were Dea. Edgar Damon—a lineal descendant of Dea. John Damon, one of the first deacons of this church,— and Dea. T. T. Briggs. The first named gentleman responded :

Mr. President, Ladies and Gentlemen : We thank you most heartily, in behalf of the Old South Church in Reading, for your kind invitation to this bountiful collation, and these most interesting exercises. The Daughter with glad heart comes to greet her revered Mother, who, with kindly hospitality, welcomes us to the old homestead, and the festivities of this hour.

As we sit here and look upon this family party, our hearts are warmed as the events of the past are brought to our minds. The permanent good this church has accomplished may be seen in these added churches, their usefulness, and untold influences for good.

This ancient structure, how well it stands ; its foundations how firm— laid deep and broad upon the solid Rock. Every post erect and strong, every brace sustaining its part ; no decay is here ; it has stood the trial of centuries, showing,

"How well our God secures the fold,
Where his own flock have been."

Mr. President, the Old South Church, 106 years old, is still full of vigor and courage, and comes to this maternal board with something of pride and real joy, as she looks upon her own daughters settled by her side—the Baptist, Bethesda, Methodist and Presbyterian churches, each doing faithful service for Christ. And now, sir, thanking you for a place in these commemorative exercises, I close with this sentiment : May the Mother Church, "tried and true," "still bring forth fruit in her old age."

It is a sentiment of Scripture that "children's children are the crown of the old." Churches may sometimes look proudly upon their grand-daughters, and say, "Ye are our crown." This pleasure is permitted to us this evening; and we challenge any other ecclesiastical matron to point to a brighter crown than the Bethesda church.

Sumner Weston, Esq. responded, expressing congratulations and warm feelings of regard on the part of the large church he represented.

Unity in variety is a universal law. We both recognize and rejoice in it, and we count it a cause for special thanksgiving that Christian brethren, while disagreeing upon some points, may yet stand together upon the platform of fundamental truth. Like almost every ancient church, this one has witnessed the departure of members for opinion's sake. While regretting the absence of those brethren, we yet respect their fidelity to their convictions. We welcome them upon this commemorative occasion with the cordiality of brethren. We rejoice in their prosperity, and bid them God-speed in their work. We look for a response, to our guests from the Baptist church.

The Baptist church was represented by Rev. R. M. Nott, Brethren A. G. Sweetser, Edward Mansfield and A. N. Sweetser. The gentleman first named responded:

The response to this sentiment would most appropriately come from the pastor of the church, Rev. Dr. Keyser, or from our venerable brother, Rev. Jonas Evans, who, if present, might not merely, as one of its oldest and most beloved members, represent our church, but would also undoubtedly be welcome as one connected intimately with a number of the oldest families in the town, and one whose memory is a storehouse filled with interesting recollections of the religious history of the place. But the absence from town of the former, and the ill health of the latter, have caused the duty of replying to this courteous and fraternal sentiment to be committed to one less qualified. Yet I possess one peculiar qualification, in that, while a real and complete Baptist, I am also linked—I suppose by an inseparable bond—with the Congregationalists. The water of consecration, the "seal of the covenant," was duly placed upon my brow in infancy by the hands of my father, at that time a Congregational pastor, and I was of course, by that ceremony, made a member of a Congregational church, in that sense in which the "children of the church" are members. As I have never been notified of my dismission, or excommunication, undoubtedly I am still a member. I hope I shall receive due watch-care.

But it is worthy of being remembered on this occasion, that Baptist churches are, in reference to one of the things that most affect church character, themselves members of the *family* of Congregational churches. Our form of church government is substantially the same with yours. Our polity is not the Prelatic, nor the Presbyterian, but the Congregational. Besides, we had, to a considerable extent, a common origin with you. As regards our English development, we were, like your denomination, a part of the Puritan stock which arose to contend against the corruption and tyranny of the ecclesiastical establishment in England. In this country our independent development at first struggled against an obstacle in the theocratic institutions which the noble, but of course not properly enlightened, forefathers of New England thought it their right and duty to establish; and in the fact that, in respect to some of our denominational principles, we were found to be even protestants against the Protestants. But we are now seen to be only standing side by side with you, in relation to two most fundamental matters: first, as to the defence of what has come to be universally recognized in America as the true Protestant theory of the proper relations of civil government to religion and the rights of conscience—a theory which, established as it seems to be, American Protestants generally may yet be called upon to maintain strenuously against a dangerous assaulting force; and, secondly, what is better, in relation to the support and the universal propagation of a true, evangelical Christianity.

The Baptist church in Wakefield congratulates this church on its age, its growth in the past, and the prosperity it now enjoys; and desires the continuance of warm fraternal relations on the basis of mutual Christian confidence and love.

The charity of the Gospel is a beautiful mantle, and as broad as it is beautiful. When the Universalist churches were formed in New England they asked for a larger charity among christians; and if they arraigned existing churches as having too little, they did but emphasize a truth which men are prone to neglect. We are glad to have with us the newly-settled pastor of the Universalist church, from whose lips the Gospel, as understood by himself and his brethren, is receiving a vigorous and faithful exhibition.

Response by Rev. Quincy Whitney:

He congratulated the Pastor and Parish on the occasion which had called the company together; and thought it something to stimulate and encourage any church, that it had such a history behind it, and embodied in its present condition so much sweet christian fraternity. He rejoiced that the day had dawned when all the churches regarded "the charity of the gospel" as "a broad and beautiful mantle," and that they could now recognize in it more than formerly, some common ground of Christian Union. He saw in it the more hopeful day for the world; and instead of tearing each other in pieces, by theological weapons, they would all take the "sword of the spirit" and march hand and shoulder to victory. There was some common ground on which they could all stand, notwithstanding their theoretical differences, and that is the spirit of charity and toleration, and the vital principles of what makes the real Christian. He illustrated this point and the position of the different sects, by saying they might all be represented by taking some vials and filling them with water, and coloring each differently. One color should represent one sect, another a different sect, &c., through the catalogue. The coloring in each was the theological view which each put upon the Bible—while the basis of all these different compounds is *water*. Each church has something of the "water of life," and should not think more of its shade of theological differences, than of the water itself.

Among denominations of Christians, our Methodist brethren have no superiors for zeal; and their zeal has been repaid by a wonderful growth. When their church in this town was established, it received from this the right hand of warm fellowship, and we have seen no reason to withdraw it. We take pleasure in congratulating them upon the success of their efforts, and wish them a still greater degree of it.

The Rev. John Peterson, pastor of the Methodist church, was unavoidably absent.

The Diaconate of the First Church—illustrated in the past by many pious and saintly names; represented in the present by devoted christian men.

Response by Dea. George R. Morrison :

It is true that the office of Deacon in this church has been filled by many saintly men. The number who have served it in that capacity is now forty; and the service of some of them extended over very long terms. When I came to this town, more than forty years ago, I attended meeting at this church, and my mind reverts to those days with vivid recollections of the leading men of that time, especially the deacons. There were Dea. Bryant, Dea. Eaton, Dea. Oliver, Dea.

Boardman, Dea. Norcross, and Capt. Thomas Emerson; now all gone to their rest. The kind words that I received from each of them still linger in my mind, giving me a great degree of pleasure. May their mantle fall upon us, that we may be able to discharge our duties as faithfully as those servants of the Lord did in their day. My sentiment is, that this church may in coming years send out more branches than she has already sent forth. And may her graces shine out, that she may be a beacon light to many a wandering pilgrim.

The Gould Family—Said to be "very set in their ways," it should be added to their honor, that they are almost always SET in the right WAY. One excellent scion of the race is well SET at the head of our large and growing Sabbath school, and is a Deacon beside.

Response by Dea. J. G. Aborn:

MR. PRESIDENT: To your sentiment my feelings and reason respond. It is even so—stern, inflexible, stubborn sometimes, it may be, is the family, the race. How can this family trait be better regulated and employed than in the work of the church and sabbath school—an institution acknowledged by every christian sect and denomination to be good, affording the purest instruction, the sweetest associations, the holiest principles; thus drawing for us wisdom from the past, and hope for the future. This school was founded in the year 1818, by earnest men and women. Most of them I must have known, as it is more than forty years since I became a member. There have been eleven Superintendents. Dea. Aaron Bryant, the first elected, held the office not less than thirty years. His name, ability, faithfulness, and devotion to evangelical truth and every vital interest of the school, should be handed down from father to son, to the latest generation. His successors have followed nearly the same methods which were employed in the beginning, finding them wise and efficient in making this a school full of life and interest; and I rejoice to be able on this commemorative occasion to report—that which no one, I think, will call in question—that never, in the long history of the church, parish, or sabbath school, were we, in all respects, in a more happy and prosperous condition; and we trust in God, that He will raise up men of faith and courage, who "count not their lives dear to them," so that Christ and His cause shall be effectual in the salvation of sinners.

The following sentiment was furnished by the Pastor:

The Eaton Family—One of the oldest, most numerous and most honorable, it has furnished some of the wisest of our public servants. To none of these is the town more indebted than to one who, at the close of a life of wide usefulness, gave to it an accurate, complete and invaluable Town History—The Hon. Lilley Eaton. We miss his ever welcome presence; but we hold in lasting and grateful memory his pure character, his worthy example, and his arduous services.

Response by Henry L. Eaton, Esq. of Swampscott:

Mr. President, former Pastor, and Friends: I thank you heartily for the privilege of responding to the sentiment just given.

You have referred in words of eulogy to one who for a lifetime gave of the best he had, whether of time, talent, or labor, and at the last, I cannot help thinking, life itself, to his native town. Sir, Lilley Eaton loved with no common love, the place that gave him birth. It was to him the dearest spot on all the earth; and of all her sons, I believe none ever accomplished more than he, for her past, present, and future prosperity. Standing here on this centennial occasion—my own life measuring just half of it—I miss the familiar countenances of many whom, for long years, I remember as associates of my honored father. Their descendants are before me; and to you, companions of my childhood, and friends of later years, I extend a hearty greeting.

Members of the Congregational Church: Eighteen years ago you received my wife and myself to your fellowship and communion; and I look back to that time with feelings of gratitude which I cannot express. Precious to me are the memories of prayer meetings I have attended in the old and in the new vestry. Father Emerson and Dea. Bryant, rise before my mental vision; and I bless the Lord that He ever called me into his kingdom. Thanking you all for this opportunity of meeting you once more, I offer the following sentiment—

Members of this Church who have gone before—May their Christian graces live in us.

———

The Cowdrey Family—From William Cowdrey, one of the earliest settlers,—Deacon, Selectman, Representative, and of rare clerkly skill, as deeds and records even now attest,—down to the present time, the stock has not degenerated; and the latest descendant, emulating the virtues of his progenitor, even excels him in beauty of chirography, and may yet be a Deacon.

Response by Waldo E. Cowdrey, Esq:

Mr. President, Ladies and Gentlemen: Deacon Cowdrey was a farmer, a son of the soil, who got his living by tilling it, as his descendants in this town have to the eighth generation. But I do not propose to tell you "what I know about farming," and will only say that I hope his family may always have the right to place on their coat of arms the plough as well as the pen. Born at the opening of the 17th century, in the reign of good Queen Bess, he belongs to the epoch of Shakspeare and the Spanish Armada. I am unable to give you his opinions upon the English poet or the Spanish pirates; but as actions speak louder than words, we learn his views on two important matters. In early manhood he heard the voice of some Greeley of that day saying, "Go West, young man:" but (and I call the attention of all young men to the fact) he got married before he went West. One other thing we learn from his record—he paid his passage over, and I trust his example of paying his way may be followed by all his children.

Mr. President, I hope this ancient church may always have on its roll of members some who bear the names of its founders; but I also hope that in the future, as in the past, its burdens may be borne, and its honors shared, by many new ones—strangers to our fathers, but not strangers to their faith.

The Bancroft Family—including Deacons, Captains, Esquires, Doctors of Divinity, Historians and Judges. Eminent in the past. MORE eminent to-day.

The Temple Family—illustrious for their virtues and their ancestry, leading back to an English lineage, which includes such names as Lord Chatham, Lord Grenville and Lord Palmerston.

Judge Solon Bancroft of Reading, replied for both of the last named families; expressing his pleasure in being a sharer in the exercises of the occasion, and his increasing admiration for the heroic, wise and self-denying men who have preceded us.

The Poole Family—in our early history, distinguished for wealth, talents, and integrity,—some worthy descendants are still among us.

Response by Dr. Alexander Poole:

This is not the place to go into the history and biography of the Pooles. I can only give a few general facts concerning them.—John Poole, the ancestor of all of the name in this vicinity, and, it is believed, in Maine and Connecticut, was among the first settlers of this town; and the name came to be among the most numerous on the list of citizens; and, as far as is known, they were among the wealthiest, and, *as a consequence*, the most *respected* class of citizens. Among them are found a goodly number of *Captains, Lieutenants, Justices of the Peace, Deacons*, and one for several years Town Clerk. Two graduated from Harvard College, and one settled as a clergyman in Nova Scotia. John, the first of the name, built the first mill in town, on the site where now stands the *Wakefield Rattan Factory*; thus while replenishing his own coffers, he furnished the grain in a form acceptable to the stomachs of his neighbors. But, alas! From being numerous and influential, they have sadly degenerated, until now only two of the name remain in town of all that numerous race.

The Emerson Family—numerous, respected and influential, but especially noted for its ministers and military men, among whom may be named Rev. Joseph Emerson of Mendon, Rev. Dr. Brown Emerson of Salem, Rev. Reuben Emerson of South Reading, Rev. Alfred Emerson of Lancaster, and Rev. Thomas A. Emerson of Braintree; Capt. Thomas Emerson, of Revolutionary fame, and Capt. Thomas Emerson, whose form and voice have been so often seen and heard in this place, and who, full of years, has lately passed to his rest.

Response by Capt. James F. Emerson:

Our Ancestors—May their descendants ever follow them in those paths of life filled with good deeds and noble examples, and may the light of this (their) church, at the end of an additional 232 years, continue to reflect the beams of gospel light, repeating the proclamation: "Fear not, for behold, I bring you good tidings of great joy, which shall be to all people."

We have among us a venerable and respected gentleman of our own communion, and one who loves sweet sounds; directly connected by blood, though not by name, with some of the oldest and worthiest families of Reading, being a lineal descendant of Rev. Samuel Haugh, Dea. Thomas Nichols, Capt. John Herbert and Dea. John Goodwin—Need I name James Eustis, Esq.?

Response by Mr. Eustis:

My earliest ancestors in this town were Nathaniel Goodwin and Richard Nichols, who came here more than two hundred years ago. I am doubtful whether I can claim descent from Rev. Samuel Haugh; but that there were Deacons in my line is quite true. My memory goes back seventy-four years, and I can recollect distinctly, looking upon the remains of Mr. Prentice in his coffin. I can remember the ordination of Mr. Emerson in the following year. Mr. Eaton mentions in his history the feat of the Negro Doss, in lifting one of the great pieces of granite when this church was built. I remember "Old Doss." He was a man of great and powerful frame. When the old church was repaired, and the sounding-board was taken down, I bought it, and kept it in my barn for years as a memento of old times: but it was rather cumbersome, and was taken to pieces. In your toast you allude to my love for sweet sounds. I have such a love, and for many years enjoyed public worship in the gallery with the singers. I love my native town, and am glad that the rising generation find pleasure in thinking of the fathers.

———

Among the honored names of the early church of the first Parish, are found those of Thomas and Susannah Hartshorne, and later, that of James Hartshorne, for over twenty years a deacon of this church—a numerous and respected race, noted for their intelligence and good looks.

Response by Jacob C. Hartshorne, Esq. :

Mr. President, Ladies and Gentlemen,—As I look down the long, dim path of years, and view the noble deeds and memorable names so thickly strewn therein, I feel how weak and inadequate will be the words which come at my command, in response to this noble sentiment. But, sir, I cannot conceal the honest pride I feel in the fact that, among the founders of this ancient church and town, my ancestors bore a helpful and honorable part. Time would fail me to speak of all, from Thomas down to James; but that they were useful, energetic, tried and true, is well attested by the record of their eventful lives as members of the church and State; and although none of them acquired great wealth, they have thus far been able, all of them, to *blow their own horn.* But "art is long, and time is fleeting," and remembering your injunction to be brief, I beg leave to close my remarks by offering this sentiment, expressive of the spirit of our ancestors:

Liberty! —'Tis Liberty alone that gives the flower of fleeting life its lustre and perfume: and we are weeds without it.

——

The great family of Brown—It has reflected honor on the old town, from Nicholas Brown, the first settler, through Deacons, Generals, Captains, and Esquires. The blood is well preserved, though the name has become scarce in our Society.

Response by T. J. Skinner, Esq:

Having been requested to respond to the foregoing toast, in behalf of wife and children, I have found upon consulting our valuable Town History, that my family are direct descendants of the veritable Nicholas mentioned in the toast—being only the seventh and eighth generation removed, and coming down as follows, viz.: from Nicholas to Josiah, to Josiah again, to Nathaniel, to Jacob, to Pearson, to John Brown, 2nd, who was the father of my wife. Said Nicholas came over from England, and first settled in Lynn, but soon removed to this town, where he resided upon the place now occupied by E. A. Upton, Esq., and also upon the estate now owned by Lucius Beebe, Esq. General Benjamin Brown, of Revolutionary fame, was also a descendant of Nicholas, through another son—Joseph. He was an eminent and influential citizen of this town for many years. He was by trade a tanner. He was also a soldier in the Revolution, Colonel in the Continental army, General in the militia, Town Clerk, Selectman, Representative, delegate to the 1st Provincial Congress, and last—which in those times was considered highest of all—became a deacon in the church. Still another branch of the Brown family is the family residing in the east part of the town, of which the late W. L. Brown, Esq., was a part. They also descended from Nicholas, through another son—Cornelius. As suggested in the toast, the name of Brown, although so common, has become somewhat scarce in our own society. The only persons left of our own family to continue the name, are the two children of the late Hervey W. Brown, and the children of the late Charles B. Brown.

The Aborn Family—Though not among the first settlers of Reading, they early flourished in our sister town of Lynnfield, and have long been firmly rooted in our soil. Their record is good, and may the blood and name be perpetuated—BY GEORGE, (if not by others.)

Response by George W. Aborn, Esq.:

One of the number who formed the first church in Lynnfield was Dr. John Aborn. His son Samuel, who was Deacon in the same church, was my grandfather. Aborns are few in number, but have always been found filling various offices in the church and parish.

Joseph Damon, the worthy son of an honored father, Dea. John Damon. He left us 200 years ago, and has only just returned in the person of his very great grandson, the precious fame of whose services in the cause of Christ and Humanity, is world wide—the Seaman's Friend, Rev. Dr. Samuel C. Damon of Honolulu.

Response by following letter:

WORCESTER, June 20, 1876.

C. W. EATON, Esq

MY DEAR SIR:—Your letter of yesterday has this moment been received, and I hasten to reply, expressing my sincere and heartfelt regret that my previous engagements will not allow me to be present on the interesting occasion referred to, or even to visit again the good old town of Reading.

Please assure all gathering on Wednesday evening at your *Centennial Service*, of my cordial good will, and the honor which I so much value of being connected with the original settlers of Reading, and especially being thus connected with one of the very earliest Deacons of the Church, and his wife *Abigail*.

On returning to my far-away home in the Pacific, I shall look back with an honest pride to Reading, associating the names of *Reading, Dedham*, and *Holden*, with that of *Honolulu*, where I have spent more than one third of a century in preaching the gospel, and where I hope to finish my ministry, when it shall please the Master, who commissioned his disciples to "go into all the world, and preach the gospel to every creature." Most truly yours, SAMUEL C. DAMON.

The Upton Family—They are LONG in the land, and well UP in the world.

E. A. Upton, Esq., responded:

MR. PRESIDENT:—I cannot speak with much knowledge for the members of the family who have been long in the land, and I am altogether too modest a man to speak for those who are well up in the world, for I presume the sentiment measured them by long measure, and not by any standard of position: therefore I am doubtful if you have made a judicious selection in the person to represent them this evening. I was educated and trained to believe that the religion of this church was the only religion capable of carrying a person through this world into a life of repose and happiness: but as I desire to maintain the reputation of the family for obeying Biblical precepts, I have left this ancient society for one equally confident in the saving qualities of its religion, that I might cleave unto my wife; but the change has not erased or destroyed the early impressions which I received, however darkly they may appear in my daily life. It is a pleasure for me to meet with you in this social manner, and bring to mind the pleasant traditions, associations and reminiscences which surround this ancient church; and although it does not appear that many of the later members of the family have been connected with it, yet it is well to know that many of them were active and influential in the society which was a daughter of this church, and settled in the cold regions of North Reading, and through their influence and active works, that society grew in strength and increased in numbers, until it has become a beacon light in the galaxy of churches. May the future light of this church be equal in brightness and power to that which it has shed in the past, and may it continue to exercise a controlling influence over all upon whom it shines.

The Law—properly administered, the bulwark of our rights.

C. P. Judd, Esq., of Reading, responded :

The Puritans had great regard for "law and order." Before they landed from the Mayflower they made a written compact of government. They treated the Indians fairly and honestly. Shortly after their arrival, they found a pile of Indian corn in the custody of no one: they used it, but immediately hunted up the owner, and paid him for it. They paid the Indians for every foot of land they took, up to the time of King Philip's war; and paid a fair price for the land, too—all it was worth—though the compensation was only a jewsharp. The laws of our forefathers were more humane than those of any other country in the world at that time. It is said that they were guilty of persecution. This is not so; for they only enforced their laws. It is not persecution to apply the law to a party who came to the State after the law was made, and wilfully violated it. It is said they hung the Quakers; but the Quakers were guilty of great indecency; and the rule of the Pilgrims was, "Let everything be done with decency, and in order." This, too, was the common injunction of your late pastor, Mr. Emerson. The family, the church and the State, were the three grand elements of early New England life. The family was sacred and indissoluble. The puritans had no divorce laws, and during the first century after their landing a divorce was hardly heard of. Now, the great business of our courts is to separate man and wife. The early clergymen were bold, educated and noble men. True, they eschewed lawyers, and kept them out of the country for many years. Nevertheless, the laws in the main were fairly interpreted by the clergy. Litigation was short and crisp. Punishment met crime. Fault is found with the old clergymen, because they allowed no one to vote in State matters who was not a member of the church. This caused no trouble, because soon after, they permitted every man of good moral character to join the church. Have we, in this age of *light*, any better basis of suffrage than a good moral character?

In the excellent historical address of the pastor of this church last Sunday, he said that formerly the clergy, in private and in public, indulged in spirituous liquors—as well as everybody else. That was true, but was not all of the truth. Let this be added: The clergy were the first to abandon ardent spirits; they first began the temperance reform, fifty years ago, and they have been the pioneers in this glorious reform from that day to the present time.

Should any one who was present at the gathering discover that the order of the sentiments in the foregoing report differs somewhat from that followed on the occasion itself, and that some other changes have been made, the fact is explained by saying that the effort has been, while reproducing the meeting in its main features and spirit, to give special prominence to the church in its relation to other churches, and to the families that have, from the earliest times, been identified with it.

The titles of other sentiments with the names of the respondents are as follows:

The National Government—Senator Geo. S. Boutwell; by a dispatch given among the letters printed farther on. The State Government—Thos. Winship, Esq., Representative from this town. The President of the United States—Col. John W. Locke, P. M. The Town of Reading ——. The Town of Wakefield—Hon. James Oliver, chairman of the Board of Selectmen. The Beebe Town Library—Lucius Beebe, Esq. Education—Melvin J. Hill, Principal of the High School. The Army—Maj. W. S. Greenough. The Shades of the Departed—Mrs. E. C. Poland. The Swain Family—Rev. T. A. Emerson. The Walton Family—E. H. Walton, Esq. The Uses of Tea—John F. Hartshorne, Esq. Our Triennial Bookseller—N. J. Bartlett, Esq. The Musical Sentiment—Solon Walton, chorister of the church.

The Influence of Woman—James O. Boswell, Esq. The responses it is now quite impossible to print, inasmuch as some failed at the time, and others were not reported.

It was a matter of regret that several gentleman formerly. or at present, identified with the church, could not be present. Among this number were Dr. Samuel Hart of Brooklyn, Rev. T. A. Emerson, pastor at Braintree, and Rev. W. S. Hawkes, pastor at Fairhaven, all of whom were sons of this church. Rev. Alfred Emerson, a former pastor, was compelled to be absent. From other friends of the church, who would have been gladly welcomed, the committee received the following

LETTERS:

The first is from our national historian, the Hon. George Bancroft.

NEWPORT, June 30th, 1876.

MY DEAR SIR:

Absence for nearly a week has delayed my answer to your favor of the 15th inst. I am heartily glad that you have caught the historical fever, and trust you will do good service in setting in a bright light the great deeds of our New England ancestry, who are never enough to be respected and honored.

The only matter in church history, relating to Reading, which has impressed itself on my mind, relates to the controversy in Northampton between Jonathan Edwards and the people of that town. When the greatest of New England's theologians fell into a deplorable controversy with the people of that town, and a council was called to pass upon the question of his dismission from his ministry to them, Edwards had to look far in quest of friends on whose vigor of character and independence he could rely. It was among the members of your church that he found one of his strongest supporters. That man was the father of my father—Deacon Samuel Bancroft. This fact was brought more closely to my consideration by my long residence in Northampton, within sight of the house of Edwards, and the shade trees which he planted. It has always given me satisfaction to know that the delegate sent by your church exerted all his influence and fixedness of purpose to retain Jonathan Edwards in the lovely town in which he delighted to dwell, and from which he never should have been driven.

It is possible that this incident may have escaped you; if so, I am glad to remind you of it. I remain, my dear sir, with the greatest respect,

Very truly yours,
GEORGE BANCROFT.

REV. CHARLES R. BLISS.

From Ex-Governor John A. Dix, of New York, the following was received:

NEW YORK, June 16th, 1876.

DEAR SIR:

I have just received your favor. Anthony Dix, who came to Plymouth in the second vessel that reached there after the first landing of the Pilgrims, was the common ancestor of Ralph Dix and myself, and I remember Reading as the residence of one branch of the family; but, in the absence of the records, I cannot say which.

I should be very happy to be with you on the 21st inst. if it were in my power; but as it is not, you will oblige me by making me known to those who may be assembled on the occasion, as one who, though absent, takes a cordial interest in their proceedings. I am, dear sir,

Respectfully and truly yours,
JOHN A. DIX.

REV. CHARLES R. BLISS.

Senator Geo. S. Boutwell, descended from the Boutwells who were among the early settlers of this town, sent from a distant State, where he was serving upon a committee of the United States Senate, the following telegraphic dispatch:

JACKSON, MISS., June 20th, 1876.

REV. CHARLES R. BLISS, WAKEFIELD:

If I were in Massachusetts I should attend your gathering, that I might revive and increase my veneration for the Founders of our Commonwealth, who also established the institutions of religion, education and liberty, to which the country owes its existence and character.

GEO. S. BOUTWELL.

From Rev. John W. Chickering, D. D.:

"LAKESIDE," WAKEFIELD, June 20th, 1876.

REV. CHARLES R. BLISS:

Dear Sir and Brother:—I am sorry not to be with you all tomorrow. I am fond of anniversaries, centennials, and memorials. I especially like church commemorations. Our church is connected with some of my earliest recollections. My memory hardly runs so far back as to Father Emerson's settlement, at which, I believe, my father assisted; but of Father Emerson himself, and of his boys and girls, I have a very vivid recollection, including his deep and rich baritone voice, more agreeable in singing than in the occasional gentle reproofs which his children or their young visitors may have *sometimes* needed; not that

74

he was *a scolding* man, by any means, but even *ministers'* children may do wrong.

At a later period, I have pleasant recollections of stage rides along the beautiful lake-shore—i. e. "side of the *pond*"—wishing I could live in so pretty a spot. Then came a trying time to me, and I fear, more so to this congregation—August 9th, 1829, when, a boy of twenty-one, I preached my first two sermons as a full fledged licentiate, in the pulpit, and, worse still, in the *presence* of the venerable pastor, kind, but sound and observant, and with only too good a field for his critical judgment.

Now, for nearly ten years I have dwelt among the children and children's children of that congregation, and other families, like my own, new-comers. So I send my cordial greetings to you, as one *of* you, with the hope that our children and children's children may not have reason to be ashamed of us; while they shall exceed both us and our fathers in all that goes to make good citizens and good christians.

Yours, all, with regards and regrets,

JOHN W. CHICKERING.

Per Type-writing-machine. Not in use in our fathers' days.

From Daniel Allen, Esq. :

RUMNEY, N. H., June 20th, 1876.

BELOVED PASTOR:

Your kind letter was received yesterday. I was glad to learn that you were to have a social Centennial gathering of our church and congregation. I need not say to you how much pleasure it would give us to be with you, but we shall have to forego it.

There is no nation but ours, and no community but New England, that has such a glorious history, and such rich and interesting material for centennials and re-unions. The high and holy motives which actuated our Christian ancestors in laying the foundations of our country and its institutions, are worthy of everlasting remembrance. How appropriate, then, for our ancient church in Wakefield, which has stood so long, and is so true a witness for the "faith once delivered to the saints," to review its history, to gather instruction from our pious fathers "who lived and walked with God."

I will give in closing the following sentiment:

The keynote of our Pilgrim Fathers—The Bible and Free Schools. The history of one hundred years has given sufficient evidence that no substitute for them has been found, as the ground of a nation's prosperity, or of true and genuine civilization.

Yours truly,

DANIEL ALLEN.

REV. CHARLES R. BLISS.

CONCERNING THE PRESENT USAGES, RULES AND
INSTRUMENTALITIES OF THE CHURCH AND
PARISH, WITH THE NAMES OF THE
MEMBERS OF EACH.

THE CHURCH.

PRINCIPLES AND RULES.

1. This church is independent in its internal organization and management. It controls the admission, discipline and removal of its members, according to its own conception of the law of Christ. It will, however, extend to sister Congregational churches, and receive from them, fellowship, advice and assistance.

2. ADMISSION AND TRANSFER OF MEMBERS.—Candidates for membership meet the Church Committee, not to undergo a rigid examination, but to state their reasons for believing themselves to be Christians. They receive each a copy of the Church Confession, and if they express no dissent from it before the Sabbath of their public reception, they are held to have endorsed it. They also prepare a brief statement of their experience, to be read at the preparatory lecture, at which time a vote of admission, conditioned upon their taking the Covenant upon the Sabbath following, and upon their receiving or having received Baptism, will then be taken.

Members of other churches, enjoying church privileges with us, are desired to present letters at an early date; and such letters alone, except for special reasons, shall entitle them to a membership in this body.

Members of this church who remove their residence from this place, are expected to transfer their relation to some other church within two years after leaving us, applying for letters of dismission in writing. And if, after having been notified of this rule, absent members shall refuse or neglect to ask such letters, and fail to give adequate reasons for the omission, the church may withdraw from them its watch and care.

3. RIGHTS AND DUTIES OF MEMBERS.—Every member has a right to church privileges till he forfeits it, and, when accused of misconduct, he has a right to know the definite charges made against him, and to have an open and candid trial.

Every member is under solemn obligation to promote the peace, purity and prosperity of the church. Should any member feel aggrieved by the conduct of another, he should heed the injunction of Christ contained in Matthew XVIII: 15-17. Should any member wish to join another church, he should ask in a proper spirit to be dismissed from this. Should any member adopt religious views radically different from those held by us, and, blameless of any other offence, forsake our communion, the church may withdraw fellowship from such person without taking the usual steps of discipline, and thenceforth his relative position shall be like that of one who had never joined us.

4. CHURCH CENSURES.—This church regards immoral conduct, breach of express covenant vows, and neglect of acknowledged religious duties, as offences subject to censure; and the several censures of the church are: private reproof, public admonition, suspension from church privileges, and excommunication.

5. OFFICERS.—*The permanent officers* of this church are the Pastor or Pastors, and four Deacons. The Pastor is elected by the church in conjunction with the parish. The Deacons are chosen by the church, and hold their office as the church may direct. *The annual officers* are a Clerk, a Treasurer, and a Church Committee. The Clerk shall keep the church record. The Treasurer, who shall be a Deacon, shall manage the pecuniary affairs of the church, subject to the direction of the board of Deacons, who shall authorize all expenditures, and audit all accounts. The Treasurer shall present to the church a yearly report. The Church Committee shall consist of the Pastor and five lay brethren, whose duty it shall be to receive the statements of those wishing to join the church, and report to the church the names of candidates approved by them, to look after the spiritual interests of the brotherhood, and to be the organ through which matters of discipline shall be presented to the church.

6. COMMITTEE UPON THE SABBATH SCHOOL.—There shall be chosen annually a Committee of three, to act as a medium of communication between the church and Sabbath School. In connection with the Pastor and Superintendent, they shall seek to bring the School into close connection with the church; devise ways and means to replenish the library, and render in all possible ways such assistance as the best interests of the School may require.

STANDING REGULATIONS.

1. The annual meeting for the choice of officers shall be held in January, at such time as the Pastor and Deacons may appoint. Every business meeting shall be notified from the pulpit on the Sabbath preceding the meeting, and such a meeting shall be called whenever five members express in writing their desire that one should be held.

2. All officers shall be chosen by ballot.

3. The church will celebrate the Lord's Supper on the first Sabbath afternoon of January, March, May, July, September and November, and, ordinarily, baptism will be administered on those occasions. Preparatory Lecture will be preached at some time during the previous week.

4. Candidates for admission will be propounded, ordinarily, two weeks before their reception.

5. The Pastor shall preside in all meetings of the church. In his absence, the duty shall be discharged by the senior Deacon present.

6. All business meetings shall be opened with prayer.

The foregoing Rules may be changed by a vote of two-thirds of the members present at any legal meeting.

78

CONFESSION OF FAITH.

ADOPTED SEPTEMBER 30, 1765, AND USED ACCORDING TO RULE 2ND, UNDER THE HEAD OF PRINCIPLES AND RULES.

1. We believe in one eternal, almighty God, the Father, Son and Holy Ghost, who created the world by his power, and governs it by his providence, and is the Redeemer of the fallen world by His Son, Jesus Christ.

2. We believe the holy Scriptures of the Old and New Testament to be the word of God, and adhere to them as the only rule of faith and practice, directing us in all matters of divine worship, and in Church-administration, as well as in an holy life and conversation.

3. We believe that our first parents fell from that estate of integrity, honor and happiness, in which God at first created them, and that all mankind fell in them by their transgression in eating the forbidden fruit, and that thereby they involved themselves and their posterity in a state of sin and death; and that in consequence hereof, all the generations of Adam are born in a state of corrupted nature, destitute of original righteousness and purity, under the curse of a broken law, and so rendered liable to all the miseries of this life, to death itself, and all the pains of hell forever. And that God hath from all eternity chosen a certain number of lapsed or fallen mankind to life and salvation as the end, and faith in Christ and holiness as the means.

4. We believe that God, in compassion to the sinful, perishing state of mankind, fore-ordained, and in the fullness of time sent, His only begotten Son, to be the Saviour of the world; and that Jesus Christ, the Son of God, became true and real man, being made of a woman, and in all things like unto his brethren, sin only excepted; and at the same time in his original nature, God over all, blessed forevermore; being God and man in one person.

5. That Christ the Son of God having, in compliance with his Father's will, taken on him the nature of man, hath therein substituted himself, to bear our sins in his sacrifice on the cross for the expiation of them, and humbled himself in his obedience unto death for our redemption, whereby he has made a true and perfect satisfaction to God for the sins of man.

6. That he rose again from the dead on the third day, and ascended into heaven as our victorious Redeemer, and sitteth at the right hand of God, making intercession for us, and having power given him over all things in heaven and on earth.

7. That he sustains and executes the three-fold office of Prophet, Priest, and King in his Church.

8. That in the exercise of his office as Redeemer, and of the fullness of power committed to him, he has published the gospel covenant; requiring faith and repentance of sinful men, in order to pardon and salvation; and we must look to be pardoned and saved only through the merits of Christ, applied by faith as our only available plea before God in opposition to all works, not only those of the *Mosaic* law, but all works of righteousness, which we are supposed to have done, or can do, either before or after grace received; and the only solid ground of the imputation of the righteousness of Christ to us for our justification, is our union to Christ by faith, and not works of obedience, though a lively faith, uniting to Christ, will be ever followed with works of gospel obedience.

9. We believe the Holy Spirit is given through the merit and intercession of Christ, to make application of his purchased Redemption to men's souls; and that his gracious influences are necessary to a life of faith and obedience; and particularly the regenerating and renewing power and grace of the Holy Spirit are necessary to quicken sinners naturally dead in sin, impotent, and averse to all spiritual good; and to lead them into the life of God; and his gracious aids are to be sought and depended on by believers in all their acts of the spiritual life, whereby they are enabled to persevere to perfection.

10. That Christ hath instituted a gospel ministry, and the two sacraments of Baptism and the Lord's Supper, as the outward means of the application of Redemption, to be observed in his Church till his second coming.

11. We believe in another life after this life, and that Christ will come again, and raise the dead, and judge the world; and that we must all appear before the judgment seat of Christ.

12. That at the last day, the wicked shall be adjudged to everlasting punishment, and the righteous to life eternal.

The above Calvinistic Articles of Faith we receive as being agreeable to the word of God, and the common, received opinion of these Churches.

COVENANT

You, who now present yourself (selves) before the Lord, do, in the presence of the great God, and of His people, devoutly acknowledge the God of our fathers to be the only living and true God, and receive Him to be your God in covenant, giving up yourself (selves) in and through the Lord Jesus Christ, desiring and resolving to love and fear Him, and walk before Him in holiness and righteousness all the days of your life.

You also believe in the Lord Jesus Christ, the only and eternal Son of God, and Saviour of fallen man; and do receive him as the Prophet, Priest and King of your salvation, according to the everlasting gospel, depending upon him for righteousness and everlasting life.

You likewise believe in the Holy Ghost as the author of all grace and comfort, and give up yourself (selves) to him to be sanctified, comforted and guided to eternal glory.

You do also declare your belief of the holy Scriptures, the Old and New Testament, as given by inspiration of God, and the only perfect rule of faith and practice, resolving, by the help of divine grace, to walk according to this rule.

(The Ordinance of Baptism is here to be administered.)

You do also give up yourself (selves) to this Church, covenanting and promising together with us, by the assistance of divine grace, that you will walk together with us as a member (members) of the same mystical body, in all the holy ordinances of the Lord, blameless; submitting yourself (selves) to the regular exercise of the discipline of our Lord Jesus Christ, in this Church, in the way of gospel order, peace and union.—This you solemnly profess and promise.

(THE CHURCH REPLY.)

We then receive you to our holy communion, and promise, by divine help, that we will walk together with you in brotherly love and holy watchfulness, to our mutual edification, in the faith and fellowship of our Lord Jesus Christ. AMEN.

THE PARISH.

ART. 1. The annual meeting of the Parish for the election of officers shall be held in the month of March; and other meetings may be held at such times as the Assessors shall order; and it shall be the duty of the Assessors to call a special meeting of the Parish on the request of ten members of the Parish, made in writing.

ART. 2. At the annual meeting the following officers shall be chosen, viz: Moderator, Clerk, Assessors, Treasurer, Collector, and such other officers as may be required.

ART. 3. Every meeting shall be held in pursuance of a warrant, under the hands of the Assessors, directed to the Clerk, who shall record it and post a copy upon the meeting-house, to remain at least over one Sabbath before the meeting.

ART. 4. In giving notice of the hour of meeting, the Bell shall be rung twice; the first time, one hour before the time named in the warrant, and the second time at said hour for meeting.

ART. 5. The warrant shall express the time and place of the meeting, and nothing acted upon shall have any legal operation unless the subject matter thereof shall have been inserted in the warrant.

ART. 6. The Clerk, or if there is no Clerk, or if he is absent, the Assessors, or either of them, or the Treasurer or Collector shall preside in the choice of a Moderator, and a Clerk may then be chosen either *pro tempore*, or to fill a vacancy as the case may require.

ART. 7. The Clerk, Assessors, Treasurer and Collector shall be chosen by written ballots, and shall be sworn. The Moderator may administer the oath of office to the Clerk, and the Clerk to the Assessors, Treasurer and Collector; or said oaths may be administered by a Justice of the Peace.

ART. 8. Any person wishing to become a member of this Parish, must make a written application at any regular notified meeting to the Clerk, and he shall become a member on his receiving the vote of two-thirds of the legal voters present at such meeting. Or when the Parish is not in session, should any person wishing to become a member make a written application to the Clerk, he shall make it known to the Assessors, and if the Clerk together with the Assessors shall be unanimous in their opinion, in receiving such applicant, he shall be held to be a member.

ART. 9. Persons belonging to the Parish shall be held to be members until they file with the Clerk a written notice declaring the dissolution of their membership.

ART. 10. No person shall have a right to vote in the affairs of the Parish, unless he is a member thereof.

ART. 11. It shall be the duty of the Clerk to record the transactions of all meetings, record and place on file all letters and applications to the Parish, and to keep a register book in which shall be written the names of members, showing when admitted, when discharged or deceased.

ART. 12. These By-Laws may be altered or amended at any regular meeting of the Parish, the subject matter of such alterations or amendments being inserted in the warrant.

PUBLIC WORSHIP.

The church adheres to the ancient practice, and expects two sermons on the Sabbath. The services commence at 10 1-4 A. M., and 2 3-4 P. M.

Order of Services. A. M.

Doxology.	Scripture Reading.	Sermon.
Invocation.	Prayer.	Prayer.
Singing.	Te Deum Laudamus.	Singing.
	Benediction.	

Substituting an Anthem for the Doxology, and a Selection by the Choir for the Te Deum Laudamus, and dropping the Invocation, the order for the afternoon is the same.

The Missionary Concert is held on the first Sabbath evening of each month; the Sabbath School Concert on the second, and a prayer meeting on each of the remaining ones. These meetings commence at half-past six o'clock.

The Church prayer meeting is held on Tuesday evening, commencing in winter at half-past seven, in summer at a quarter before eight.

The Young People's prayer meeting, alternating at some seasons with the Pastor's Bible class, is held on Friday evening.

THE SERVICE OF SONG.

This is led by a Quartette who receive compensation, sustained by a choir, and participated in by the congregation.

Organist. Miss Mary McAllister.

Quartette.

Mr. Solon Walton, *Leader and Tenor.*   Miss E. Perkins, *Soprano.*
Mrs. Solon Walton, *Alto.*   Mr. C. Crosby, *Bass.*

Choir.

TENOR.	SOPRANO.
Mr. J. C. Hartshorne	Miss Ella M. Dager
" J. H. Hartshorne,	" Myra A. Stearns
" C. A. S. Troup	" Rosa. V. Nesmith
" Wallace Kendall	" Nellie A. Miller
" Hiram P. Flagg	" Hattie E. Perkins
	" Florence Burditt
BASS.	
" E. H. Walton	ALTO.
" Henry Haskell	Mrs Kate M. Howard
" J. F. Emerson	Miss Hattie E. Hall
" J. W. Poland	" Laura P. Flagg
" P. H. Southworth	" Annie L. Ballard
" Herbert W. Walton	
" Kingman S. Nichols	

SABBATH SCHOOL.

OFFICERS AND TEACHERS.

Superintendent.   *Asst. Superintendent.*
Dea. John G. Aborn.   George H. Maddock.

Secretary and Treasurer.
William P. Preston.

Librarians.
Harry Foster.   Wallace Kendall.   H. W. Brown.

Teachers.

Dea. A. W. Chapman	E. H. Walton
Joseph Burditt	Herbert W. Walton
G. W. Kendall	G. H. Maddock
Charles H. Stearns	Waldo E. Cowdrey
Charles F. Richardson	Jacob C. Hartshorne
Chester W. Eaton	Geo. W. Aborn
Wm. S. Greenough	E. E. Emerson
Samuel K. Hamilton	Mrs. Charles R. Bliss

Mrs. Addison Hubbard
" Eliza T. Freeman
" Charles H. Shepard
" Sarah Smith
" Charles H. Stearns
" John W. White
" L. D. Noyes

Mrs. Will. A. Blanchard
Miss Ellen Clayes
" Esther C. Allen
" Hattie A. Cate
" Addie C. Lane
" Emma E. Currier
" Nellie A. Miller

Infant Class—Miss Frances S. Clayes.

Whole membership of the School, 333.

A Union Sabbath School in Montrose draws from this church support
as follows:

Dea. George R. Morrison, *Superintendent*.

Teachers.

Joseph Burditt.   William P. Preston.   Wallace Kendall.
Mrs. E. T. Freeman.   Mrs. L. D. Noyes.   Dea. A. W. Chapman.

INSTRUMENTALITIES OF BENEVOLENCE.

Three annual collections are taken by solicitors, viz. : For the American Board, The Home Missionary Society, and The American Missionary Association. Collections for the diff' rent denominational and other Societies, are taken in the church.

The Ladies' Charitable Society labors efficiently in providing boxes for Home Missionary families, and for the needy nearer at hand.

Officers.

Mrs. T. J. Skinner, *President*.   Mrs. George H. Maddock, *V. President*.
" A. S. Atherton, *Secretary*. Miss Esther C. Allen, *Treasurer*.

Directresses.

Mrs. John T. Judkins.   Mrs. D. T. Miller.   Mrs. S. K. Hamilton.

The Woman's Missionary Society is auxiliary to the Woman's Board of Missions.

Officers.

Mrs. Charles R. Bliss, *Directress*.   Mrs. C. E. McKay, *Secretary*.
Mrs. George H. Maddock, *Treasurer*.

The Relief Committee exists, to give aid to families and persons whose
necessities require it. It is a large committee, and is subdivided into
an Executive Committee of five, and seventeen other committees, of
four each. Collections to supply funds are taken in church, and the
work is done according to the suggestions of the following card, which
is given to each member:

"BE CAREFUL TO MAINTAIN GOOD WORKS."

VISITOR'S CARD.

DISTRICT No.

STREETS

NAMES OF COMMITTEE.

SUGGESTIONS.

PRELIMINARY.—Never convey the impression that you have been
appointed to visit.

1.) Call upon our own families to ascertain who will furnish delicacies
or other assistance for the sick, and aid for the poor, on application
from you.

2.) Call upon families known not to be connected with any religious
society, and invite them to attend church, and send their children to
the S. School.

3. Call upon new residents who may be supposed to have affiliations
with us, and invite them to church.

4.) Call upon the sick, and if they need other assistance than what you
can render, report them to the Secretary and the Pastor.

5. Call upon those in straitened circumstances, and see what aid can
be judiciously rendered, and report as above.

6.) Seek out neglected children, and if they need clothing report them
to the Charitable Society, and bring them to the Sabbath School.

Give religion a place in your conversation, and endeavor to create
mutual acquaintance and sympathy among the people.

Let the committee confer together, and depute one of their number to
make a report on or near the first of each month to the Secretary of the
General Committee.

ANNUAL EXPENSES.

Whole amount for the year 1876. . . . $3,200

DISTRIBUTED AS FOLLOWS:

For Pastor's Salary,	$2,000
Church Music,	600
Services of the Janitor,	175
Miscellaneous Expenses,	425

OFFICERS AND MEMBERS OF THE CHURCH
MARCH 1, 1877.

Pastor.

CHARLES R. BLISS.

Deacons.

George R. Morrison.   Amos W. Chapman.
Cyrus N. White.   John G. Aborn.

Members.

Abbott, Mary
Aborn, Elizabeth
Aborn, John G.
Aborn, Mary E.
Aborn, George W.
Aborn, Mary F.
Allen, Daniel
Allen, Abi W.
Allen, Sarah P.
Allen, Esther C.
Allen, Mark W.
Allen, Parthina E.
Ames, Azel Jr.
Ames, Sarah D. T.
Atherton, Emma A.
Atherton, Arlon S.
Atherton, Susan M.
Atherton, William S.
Atherton, Sarah Bell

Bacon, Jane M.
Bailey, Alpha N.
Bailey, Mary F.
Ballard, William
Ballard, Hannah J.
Ballard, Annie Lucretia
Bancroft, Elizabeth R.
Bartlett, Mamie E.
Berry, Leander S.
Blasland, Gideon B.
Blasland, Melissa K.
Blanchard, Will. A.
Blanchard, M. Addie
Bliss, Charles R.
Bliss, Mary F.
Boardman, Nancy A.
Boardman, Moses
Boardman, Susan R.
Boswell, James O.
Britton, Richard
Britton, Sarah
Brown, Mary A.

Brown, Elvira J.
Bryant, Clarissa O.
Burditt, Joseph
Burditt, Florence
Butler, Mary W.

Carey, Gilman
Carey, Betsey M.
Carey, Albert C.
Cate, Hattie A.
Chapman, Amos W.
Chase, Sarah E.
Chickering, John W.
Chickering, Frances E.
Clayes, Dana
Clayes, Ellen
Clayes, Frances S.
Coffin, Annie R.
Colby, S. M. P.
Cowdrey, Waldo E.
Crane, William
Crane, Sarah A.
Currier, Hannah E.
Currier, Alonzo A.
Currier, Mary E.
Currier, Emma E.
Currier, Alice G.

Dager, Ella M.
Darling, David H.
Davis, Hannah B.
Dearborn, N. D.
Dearborn, Lucy S.
Dunshee, Sarah M.

Eaton, Chester W.
Eaton, Emma G.
Emerson, Adaline
Emerson, George
Emerson, Emily N.
Emerson, Eugene E.
Emerson, Sophia P.

Emerson, George D.
Emmons, Mary Ann
Eustis, James
Evans, Charles A.
Evans, Olive M.

Flagg, Laura P.
Flagg, Laura E.
Flagg, Hiram P.
Folsom, Helen A.
Foster, Elizabeth R.
Foster, Jonathan
Foster, Aaron A.
Foster, Rebecca T.
Foster, Caroline F.
Foster, Harry
Freeman, Eliza T.
Freeman, Dora

Gardner, Abigail B.
Gardner, Nellie M.
Gibb, James
Gibb, Esther Levina
Godfrey, Warren H.
Godfrey, Ellen K.
Gould, Louisa
Green, Susan E.
Greenough, William S.
Greenough, Elizabeth M.

Hall, Eveline N.
Hall, Jerusha
Hall, Hattie E.
Hamilton, Samuel K.
Hamilton, Annie E. D.
Hart, Hannah M.
Hart, Henry J.
Hart, L. Augusta
Hartshorne, Ida L.
Hartshorne, Jacob C.
Haskell, Henry Jr.
Haskell, Abbie M.
Hawkes, Electa B.
Hayward, John R.
Hayward, Mary Ann
Heath, Helen
Hervey, Carrie E.
Hill, Melvin J.
Hill, Louisa E.
Hobson, Sadie M.
Holt, Walter E.
Horton, Anna R.
Howard, Kate M.
Hubbard, Addison
Hubbard, Lucy A.
Hunter, Nathan A.
Hunter, Clarissa

Hutchinson, Eliza A.

Judkins, John T.
Judkins, Lucy A.

Kelton, Ada E.
Kendall, George W.
Kendall, Myra M.
Kendall, Wallace
Kilgore, Emma G.
Kimball, Stephen L.
Kimball, Asenath
Kingman, Sarah B.
Kingman, Lucy E.

Lane, David P.
Lane, Mary A.
Lane, Addie C.
Leggett, O. Annie
Linnell, Hannah C.
Locke, Elizabeth W.

Maddock, George H.
Maddock, Florence J.
Marshall, Alson L.
Marshall, Sarah A.
Marston, Otis
Marston, Hannah
Martin, Thomas J.
Martin, Julia
Martin, Annie S.
Maynell, Evelyn
McKay, Charlotte E.
Miller, Mary L.
Miller, Nellie A.
Minikin, Mary A.
Mooney, Annie I.
Moors, Sarah K.
Morrison, George R.
Morrison, Sarah E.
Morrison, S. Georgette
Moses, Elizabeth
Murray, Nellie A.

Nesmith, Rosaline V.
Nichols, Mary A.
Nichols, Emily G.
Nichols, James
Nichols, Caroline R.
Nichols, Kingman S.
Nichols, Mary C.
Nichols, George F. R.
Nichols, Annie E.
Norcross, Daniel
Norcross, Ellen
Norcross, Sarah H.
Noyes, Lucretia D.

88

Nye, Abbie F.

Oliver, Sarah
Oliver, James
Oliver, Almira S.

Parker, Samuel Jr.
Parker, Eliza L.
Perkins, Lydia K.
Perkins, Zillah E.
Perkins, Almira
Perkins, Frances O.
Perkins, Harriet E.
Pierce, Susan
Poland, Emily C.
Poland, Ella M.
Pond, Lydia A.
Potter, Martha G.
Preston, William P.
Proctor, Mattie.

Rand, Mary
Richardson, Charles F.
Richardson, Margaret I.
Richardson, Frederick E.

Savage, George
Savage, Emma
Savage, Emma
Savage, Ann Maria
Savage, Joseph G.
Savage, Harriet N.
Savage, Harriet G.
Shedd, Sarah A.
Skinner, Mary A.
Skinner, T. Judson
Skinner, Hattie E.
Smith, Nancy
Smith, Sarah
Southworth, Mason S.
Southworth, Sophia L.
Southworth, Palmer H.
Spaulding, Lucinda
Stearns, Charles H.
Stearns, Henrietta C.
Stearns, Myra A.
Stevens, Lucy H.

Stowell, Henry W.
Stowell, Mary E.
Stowell, Issachar
Stowell, Mary E.
Strong, Edward T.
Strong, Annie G.
Sweetser, Selina
Sweetser, Moses
Sweetser, Leonard
Sweetser, Delphia E.
Sweetser, Edward
Sweetser, Lizzie B.
Sweetser, Frank H.
Sykes, Margaret F.

Townsend, Jacob
Townsend, Nancy
Troup, Charles A. S.
Troup, E. E.
Tufts, Charles H.
Tufts, Emma L.

Underwood, Emily S.

Wales, Mary
Walton, Ann
Walton, Nancy
Walton, Oliver
Walton, Hannah F.
Walton, E. H.
Walton, Sarah S.
Walton, Solon
Walton, Ann Maria
Walton, Herbert W.
Walton, Rebecca T.
Weed, George C.
White, Sarah
White, Cyrus N.
White, Ruth P.
White, Selim S.
White, Edson W.
White, John W.
White, Etta May
White, Nancy
Willis, William H.
Wilson, Margaret N.
Winslow, Harvey N.

Whole membership 273.

PARISH OFFICERS FOR THE YEAR 1876, AND A LIST
MEMBERS.

James F. Emerson, *Secretary.*

T. J. Skinner, *Treasurer.*

Assessors.

George W. Aborn.   J. C. Hartshorne,   W. S. Greenoug

Committee on Music.

G. H. Maddock,   T. J. Skinner,   N. D. Dearborn.

Collector, G. R. Morrison.   *Auditor,* E. E. Emerson

Members.

Abbott, Benj. F.
Abbott, George
Aborn, George W.
Aborn, John G.
Aldrich, B. F., Jr.
Allen, Daniel
Ames, Azel, Jr.
Arrington, G. B.
Arrington, W. M.

Ballard, William
Beebe, Lucius
Blanchard, Stephen R.
Bliss, Charles R.
Boardman, E. E.
Boardman, Moses
Boswell, James O.
Britton, Richard
Burditt, George
Burditt, Joseph
Burditt, William
Burrill, A.

Carey, Albert C.
Carey, George E.
Carey, Gilman
Carpenter, George O.
Chapman, A. W.
Clark, J. H.
Corey, Charles A.
Cowdrey, Jonas
Cowdrey, W. E.
Currier, A. A.

Darling, David H.
Davies, David L.
Davis, Charles
Dearborn, N. D.

Eaton, Chester W.
Eaton, Everett W.
Eaton, Henry L.
Emerson, E. E.
Emerson, James F.
Emerson, Thomas
Emerson, Thomas A.
Evans, Charles A.
Eustis, James

Foster, Aaron

Godfrey, Warren H.
Gowing, G.
Green, Charles W.
Greenough, Wm. S.

Hamilton, Samuel K.
Hanson, M. P.
Hart, Abner B.
Hart, Henry J.
Hartshorne, John F.
Hartshorne, Henry G.
Hartshorne, Jacob C.
Haskell, Henry, Jr.
Hawkes, Geo. L.
Hayden, Wm. H.
Howe, James W.
Hubbard, Addison
Hunter, N. A.
Hurd, Francis P.

Jordan, Charles

Kendall, G. W.
Kilgore, T. W. G.

Lane, D. P.

Linnell, Geo.
Locke, John W.
Loring, G. W.

Maddock, Geo. H.
Marshall, Alson L.
Marston, E. H.
Miller, D. T.
Mitchell, R. H.
Morrison, Geo. R.

Newman, J. Frank
Nichols, James
Nichols, Samuel H.
Norcross, Daniel

Oliver, D. B.
Oliver, Henry
Oliver, James
Oliver, J. G.

Phelps, Henry
Poland, J. Warren
Poole, Alexander
Preston, William P.

Richardson, Charles F.

Savage, George

Savage, J. G.
Sawyer, F. A.
Sawtell, W. H.
Shepard, C. H.
Skinner, T. J.
Stearns, Charles H.
Stowell, Issachar
Strong, Edward T.
Sweetser, H. N.
Sweetser, Moses

Tibbetts, George E.
Tillson, J. G. W.
Towle, Jonathan
Townsend, Jacob
Tufts, Charles H.

Upton, E. A.

Wade, Francis F.
Wallis, T. R.
Walton, E. H.
Walton, Oliver
White, Cyrus N.
White, John W.
Willis, William H.
Wiley, Benjamin B.
Wiley, Francis P.

www.ingramcontent.com/pod-product-compliance
Lightning Source LLC
Chambersburg PA
CBHW020303090426
42735CB00009B/1197